Series / Number 07-001

ANALYSIS OF VARIANCE

SECOND EDITION

GUDMUND R. IVERSEN
Swarthmore College

HELMUT NORPOTH
State University of New York—Stony Brook

SAGE PUBLICATIONS
The International Professional Publishers
Newbury Park   London   New Delhi

For information:

SAGE Publications, Inc.
2455 Teller Road
Thousand Oaks, California 91320
E-mail: order@sagepub.com

SAGE Publications Ltd.
6 Bonhill Street
London EC2A 4PU
United Kingdom

SAGE Publications India Pvt. Ltd.
M-32 Market
Greater Kailash I
New Delhi 110 048 India

Printed in the United States of America

International Standard Book Number 0-8039-3001-1

Library of Congress Catalog Card No. 87-061276

02 03 04 18 17 16 15 14 13

When citing a university paper, please use the proper form. Remember to cite the Sage University Paper series title and include the paper number. One of the following formats can be adapted (depending on the style manual used):

(1) IVERSEN, G. R., and NORPOTH, H. (1976) *Analysis of Variance*. Sage University Papers Series on Quantitative Applications in the Social Sciences, 07-001. Thousand Oaks, CA: Sage.

OR

(2) Iversen, G. R. and Norpoth, H. (1976). *Analysis of variance*. (Sage University Papers Series on Quantitative Applications in the Social Sciences, series no. 07-001). Thousand Oaks, CA: Sage.

CONTENTS

106952

Series Editor's Introduction to the Second Edition

One goal of our series is to strike a balance between theory and application, equations and examples, that not only makes learning easier for many readers but also gives them a deeper understanding of the utility, appropriateness, and difficulties of using the techniques described. The first edition of Iversen and Norpoth's *Analysis of Variance* was particularly successful in this regard. Consequently, in improving the volume for this second edition, the basic structure of the text has been left undisturbed.

The authors' goal, as before, is to provide a conceptual understanding of analysis of variance. The new edition improves the presentation in various details to make the introduction to the technique especially clear. More significantly, the substantive examples are all new, including one example that is used continuously throughout the volume. This edition also places greater emphasis on the use of analysis of variance for data gathered through experiments. The presentation does not include computational formulas to be used with hand calculators; instead, references are made to the major statistical software packages, such as SPSS-X and SAS.

There is also greater emphasis here on the connection between analysis of variance and regression analysis. In several places the authors draw parallels between the two approaches (R square and eta square, collinearity and equal cell frequencies). They also show how the two procedures can be used together to detect nonlinearity, and they stress how analysis of variance and regression with dummy or indicator variables can be used interchangeably.

As the editor noted in the introduction to the first edition, this volume is valuable in its own right, but it can also serve as an introduction to more advanced topics. We especially call attention to later volumes in this series, *Analysis of Covariance*, by Wildt and Ahtola, and two recent volumes, *Multivariate Analysis of Variance*, by Bray and Maxwell, and *Multiple Comparisons*, by Klockars and Sax. Collectively, these resources can provide a good understanding of both elementary and more advanced techniques based on analysis of variance.

—*Richard G. Niemi*
Series Co-Editor

ANALYSIS OF VARIANCE
SECOND EDITION

GUDMUND R. IVERSEN
Swarthmore College
HELMUT NORPOTH
State University of New York—Stony Brook

1. INTRODUCTION

How does the public arrive at perceptions of economic well-being? This question has given rise to much speculation, discussion, and some research. One reasonable source of such perceptions is the mass media, particularly when it comes to assessments of the overall state of the economy, because this is something we as individuals do not experience directly. The question we want to study here is whether the mass media raise the public's concern with the economy by their coverage of economic news (see, e.g., Iyengar and Kinder, 1987).

In order to look for answers to this question, we design an experiment with two groups of people. Each group watches a television newscast spliced together from actual stories previously shown on the evening news. One group, known as the experimental group, watches a story on the state of the economy as part of the newscast. The other group watches the same newscast, except that the economic story has been deleted. This group is known as the control group. After watching their respective newscasts, the subjects are asked to fill out a questionnaire where they are asked, among other things, about the importance they

AUTHORS' NOTE: *We are grateful to Lawrence S. Mayer, Eric M. Uslaner, and an anonymous reader of a draft of the first edition and to an anonymous reader of a draft of the second edition for their comments.*

attach to "the state of the economy." Importance is measured on a ten-point rating scale.

People were randomly assigned to one of the groups. This is done in order to eliminate effects of other possible variables. For example, if all the young people were assigned to the experimental group and all the old to the control group, we would not know whether differences between the groups were due to age or to the difference in the newscasts they saw on television.

After the data have been collected, we have one set of values on the importance-variable for the experimental group and another set for the control group. An example of such data is shown in Table 1 in the next chapter. If the type of newscast does have an effect, the observed values should be different in the two groups; and we want to study differences between the two groups of data. One way to compare the two groups is to compare the two mean importance-values using a t-test for the difference between two means. Another way to look at the same data is to say that we have a treatment variable with two values: treatment and control. This variable is a categorical (nominal) variable. The other variable is the importance variable, and we take it to be a metric (interval) variable. The example can then be viewed as a study of the effect of a categorical variable on a metric variable. What we need is a way of statistically analyzing a relationship between variables of this kind, and analysis of variance is such a statistical method.

"Analysis of variance" is in some ways a misleading name for a collection of statistical methods and models that deal with differences in the means of a variable across groups of observations. While "analysis of means" may be a better name, the methods all employ ratios of variances in order to establish whether the means differ, and the name analysis of variance is here to stay. The name is often abbreviated to ANOVA, which a student of ours for a long time thought was the name of an Italian statistician.

The various statistical methods that fall under this name are related to other statistical methods. For example, when we study the difference between the means for only two groups of observations, as in the example above, we can find whether there is a significant difference between the means from the t-value for a difference-of-means test. This test is usually not thought of as being an analysis of variance, but we show in the next chapter that it is nothing but a special case of one of the simplest analysis of variance procedures. We show that the square of the t-value is a ratio of two variances, and this ratio gives another way of telling whether there is a statistically significant difference between the two groups.

Analysis of variance methods are also related to the set of statistical methods known as regression analysis. This point is pursued further in Chapter 5; here we note only that analysis of variance is usually the appropriate method when the groups of observations are created by a categorical independent variable. In our example the independent variable is type of newscast, and the variable has two categories (with or without economic news), resulting in two groups of observations of the dependent variable. Our task consists of determining whether the groups differ in their mean level of the dependent variable—here, importance rating. The dependent variable in an analysis of variance is almost always a metric (interval) variable.

But we can have groups formed by metric variables just as well as categorical variables. In that case analysis of variance is usually not the appropriate method for the analysis. Take education as an example of such a metric variable. When measured as number of years completed in school, all members of one group have a score of 6, all members of the next group have a score of 7, etc. With education as the independent variable, regression analysis is the appropriate way of studying whether the importance-variable or some other metric dependent variable, differs across the various education groups. Thus regression is used for the study of the effect of a metric variable on another metric variable, while analysis of variance is used for the study of the effect of a categorical variable on a metric variable. But it should be noted that the differences between analysis of variance and regression are smaller than may seem to be the case, and they can both be seen as special cases of what is known as the general linear model.

Part of the reason why regression and analysis of variance are seen as two separate sets of methods is historical. Different sciences have tended to use different types of statistical methods, and analysis of variance methods originated mostly in agriculture and the work done by the late Sir Ronald A. Fisher in the period between the two world wars. For many years he was a statistician at an agricultural experimental station in England, and a typical question he would be called upon to investigate might be whether different types of fertilizers gave different yields. Type of fertilizer is the categorical, independent variable, and yield is the metric dependent variable. By using each fertilizer on several different plots of land and measuring the yields at the end of the growing season, he would have the basis for concluding whether the fertilizers differ in their effectiveness.

Two different types of data can be analyzed using analysis of variance. The first type is experimental data, and both the television and the agricultural examples above are of this type. They have in common that the elements (people, plots of land, etc.) are randomly assigned to one of the treatments, and then the effect of the treatment is measured. The other type is observational data. In a survey we may ask people for their religious affiliation as well as their income in order to study whether income is affected by religious affiliation. This fits the pattern for analysis of variance with a categorical variable (religion) affecting a metric variable (income). All the computations are the same for the two types of data, but the difference is that with observational data, it is much harder to establish a causal effect. This is because people are not randomly assigned to different religious categories and their incomes observed later. Thus, even if we find income differences, we do not know whether they are caused by people's religion or whether they are caused by some other variable(s) that are related to religious affiliation. In experimental studies with random assignments to treatments, the effects of other variables tend to cancel each other out. Randomization was one of Fisher's major contributions to what is known as experimental design. For a further discussion of observational versus experimental research see Cochran (1965, 1983).

The formal theory of analysis of variance requires the observations to satisfy certain assumptions. There is the usual assumption that the observations have been collected independently of each other. Beyond that there are assumptions about certain quantities being additive and following the normal distribution. It is possible to use the data themselves to check on some of these assumptions, and we spell out the necessary assumptions for each method we discuss. The theory itself is heavily mathematical. We feel, rather reluctantly, that to fully understand a particular method it is necessary to understand the underlying mathematics. But it is also possible to get a very good working understanding of many of the methods without an extensive mathematical background. We present the arguments here with a minimum of mathematics, and instead we rely on intuitive and graphic arguments.

The computations needed for an analysis of variance are mostly done on computers, and we do not give computing formulas for hand calculators. If a data set is small enough that a computer is not needed, it is possible to do the computations directly from the formulas we present. But the required setup for a computer analysis is not always simple to perform, and the meaning of some of the quantities on the output are not always entirely obvious. We make an occasional reference to the SPSS-X software.

The remaining chapters take up some of the simpler analysis of variance models. We progress from one to two independent (explanatory) variables, and the resulting models are known as one-way and two-way analyses of variance, respectively. From there it is possible to go on to more than two explanatory variables. We also have to distinguish between the cases when we have observations on the dependent variable for all categories of the explanatory variable(s) and when we only have data on a subset of the categories. In the first case we have what is called a fixed model, and in the second case we have a random model. The chapters are arranged in the following way:

Ch. 2: One explanatory variable, all categories,

Ch. 3: Two explanatory variables, all categories,

Ch. 4: One explanatory variable, sample of categories,
    Two explanatory variables, sample of categories,

Ch. 5: Other models.

Further readings: After this elementary introduction to analysis of variance, it is possible to read further in standard statistical textbooks for the social sciences or other fields. For more extensive treatments on an intermediate level there are books by authors like Cochran and Cox (1957), Hays (1981), Petersen (1986), and Snedecor and Cochran (1967). The classic book on the advanced level is by Scheffé (1959).

2. ONE-WAY ANALYSIS OF VARIANCE, ALL CATEGORIES

Two groups

A t-test for the difference between two means. The fundamental ideas of analysis of variance can be understood better if we first consider in some detail the case in which the explanatory variable has only two categories. In this case the data consist of two groups of observations on the dependent variable, one group for each category of the explanatory variable. For example, we may want to study whether there is a difference in incomes between males and females, or whether there is a difference between Democrats and Republicans on some issues, and so on.

In our example on the economy we have a set of values on the rating of the importance of the economy for the control group and another set of values for the experimental group. There are five values in each of the groups, and we want to investigate whether the two groups differ on the dependent variable importance rating, denoted Y in the formulas. Specifically, we want to find out whether the mean value of the importance rating differs in the two groups. We could conclude that the groups differ if the number of observations differ, or if the standard deviations of Y differ, or if they differ in some other respect; but in analysis of variance we are concerned with whether the means differ.

One simple way to tell whether the two means differ is to compute the means and compare the two numbers. Most likely the two numbers are not the same, and that answers our question right there for the data in the sample. But, what we are more often concerned with is whether the means are different in the two populations of all possible data and not just in the observed sample. Thus we want to determine whether the observed difference between the two sample means is just due to random variations from one sample to the next, or whether the data come from populations where the means are truly different. This is another way of saying that we want to find out whether the difference between the sample means is statistically significant. Finally, even if we conclude that the population means are different, we also need to decide whether they are different enough to be of substantive importance.

These considerations are illustrated by the three different graphs in Figure 1. Graph A shows two numerically different means $\bar{y}_1$ and $\bar{y}_2$. From looking at the two means alone we cannot tell whether they are significantly different or not. In graphs B and C the difference between the two means is the same as in graph A, but graphs B and C also show the values of the five observations in each group. In graph B we see that within each of the two groups the observations are widely scattered around their respective means. Because there seems to be so much randomness in each group of data, we are inclined to say that in this case the difference between the two means is not very convincing.

In graph C the picture is different. Even though the means are the same as in graphs A and B, within each group the observations are now highly clustered. Because the observations are so clustered around the their respective means, the two groups of data seem really separated, and we conclude for graph C that the means are truly different. In this case there is a statistically significant difference between the two means.

The problem for us now becomes how to decide when means are different enough, relative to the spread of the observations in each group, to conclude that there is a statistically significant difference between the means. Analysis of variance helps us answer this question.

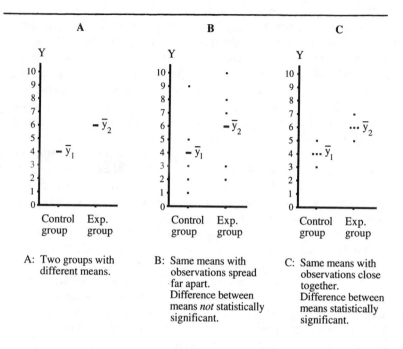

A: Two groups with different means.

B: Same means with observations spread far apart. Difference between means *not* statistically significant.

C: Same means with observations close together. Difference between means statistically significant.

Figure 1: Two Group Means with different Data

What we have to do is find a way of measuring numerically how different the means are and how much the observations are spread out around their respective means. With those two measures on hand we are then able to tell whether the means differ significantly or not. Before using analysis of variance, however, the data in graph B are analyzed in a more familiar way. Table 1 shows the data in case C and the symbols we use for the observed values of the dependent variable Y.

As already noted in Chapter 1, the t-test for the difference between two means is a special case of analysis of variance, and this t-test can be used here to investigate the difference between the two means. Denote the unknown mean of the control population as μ_1 and the unknown mean for the treatment population as μ_2. The statistical null hypothesis states that these two means are equal. The decision whether or not to reject the hypothesis is based on how likely it is that the two known sample means differ by as much as they do or more, if it really is true that

TABLE 1
Rating Scores of the Importance of the Economy,
by Type of Newscast, Hypothetical Data Case C

		Type of Newscast	
		Control Group	Experimental Group
		5	7
		4	5
		4	6
		4	6
		3	6
	Mean	4.0	6.0
In symbols:		Control Group	Experimental Group
		y_{11}	y_{21}
		y_{12}	y_{22}
		y_{13}	y_{23}
		y_{14}	y_{24}
		y_{15}	y_{25}
	Mean	$\bar{y}_1$	$\bar{y}_2$

the population means are equal. The test statistic for this hypothesis is a t-score where the numerator is

$$(\bar{y}_1 - \bar{y}_2) - (\mu_1 - \mu_2) = (\bar{y}_1 - \bar{y}_2) - 0 = 4 - 6 = -2$$

for both cases B and C. Here $\bar{y}_1$ is the sample mean for the control group and $\bar{y}_2$ is the sample mean for the experimental group. The denominator of the test statistic is slightly more complicated. First we compute the sample variance of Y in each of the two groups, which for the first group yields:

$$s_1^2 = \Sigma(y_{1j} - \bar{y}_1)^2/(n_1 - 1)$$
$$= \{(9-4)^2 + (5-4)^2 + (3-4)^2 + (2-4)^2 + (1-4)^2\}/(5-1)$$
$$= 40/4 = 10.00$$

Similarly, for the observations in the second group we get

$$s_2^2 = \Sigma(y_{2j} - \bar{y}_2)^2/(n_2 - 1) = 26/4 = 6.50$$

The denominator we seek for the t-statistic can now be found from these two variances. Because the numerator is the difference between two means, the denominator becomes the square root of the sum of the variances of the two means, that is,

$$s = \sqrt{s_1^2/n_1 + s_2^2/n_2} = \sqrt{10.00/5 + 6.50/5} = 1.82$$

The resulting ratio gives $t = -2.00/1.82 = -1.10$ with $n_1 + n_2 - 2 = 8$ degrees of freedom. The possible statistical significance of a t-value can be established from a table of the t-distribution, and this value of t is not significant.

Degrees of freedom. With five observations in each group and ten altogether, the t-value of -1.10 has eight degrees of freedom. Here is the first place where we meet the concept of degrees of freedom. This is a quantity that has confused many people. Part of the reason for this confusion is that the formal definition is heavily mathematical. Another reason is that there exists several equivalent definitions, and it is not obvious how they relate to each other.

Degrees of freedom appear any time we compute a sum of squares. One way to define the concept is to say that the degrees of freedom for a particular sum of squares is equal to the smallest number of term in the sum we need to know in order to find the remaining terms and thereby compute the sum. One would think that we need to know all the terms in order to compute a sum. But there are often restrictions imposed on the terms, and these restrictions make it possible to find some of the terms from knowing the others.

For example, the variance s_1^2 computed above is found from the sum of five squared terms. But the terms are all deviations from the mean of the original scores, and it is therefore a restriction on these terms that they add to zero. If we were told that the first four terms were 5, 1, -1, and -2, we would immediately know that the fifth term has to equal -3 since this is the only number that will make the sum of all five terms equal to zero. By squaring each of these five terms and adding the five squares we get a sum of squares equal to 40.00. Because we initially needed to know four of the five terms in order to find the sum of squares equal to 40.00, we say that this sum has four degrees of freedom. Since the sum is the numerator in the expression for the variance in the first group, we also say that the resulting variance has four degrees of freedom. When we add the two variances to get the denominator for the t-value, we also add the corresponding degrees of freedom. Here each variance is based on four degrees of freedom, and there are therefore a total of eight degrees of freedom for the t-value.

In general, with n_1 observations in one group and n_2 in another, there are n_1-1 degrees of freedom for the variance in the first group and n_2-1 degrees of freedom for the variance in the second group. When we combine the two variances to get the denominator for the t-value, we add the degrees of freedom and get a total of n_1+n_2-2 degrees of freedom for the t-value.

We have to realize, however, that when there is a certain number of terms in a sum of squares, the degrees of freedom for this sum could have as many degrees of freedom as there are terms in the sum or as few as one degree of freedom, depending on the nature of the terms in the sum. The actual determination of the correct number of degrees of freedom for a sum of squares can be difficult. The determination is sometimes simplified, however, by the fact that when two sums of squares are added, the degrees of freedom for the two sums are also added. This fact is used several times in this presentation of analysis of variance.

Equal variances. There is a requirement for this t-test that the variances in the two groups do not differ too much. In other words, s_1^2 should be approximately equal to s_2^2. As an example of what is meant by "approximately equal," we note that with five observations in each group, we can tolerate having one variance as much as six times larger than the other and still call the variances approximately equal. With more observations in the two groups, the variances have to be more equal. For example, if there are 100 observations in each of the two groups, one sample variance cannot be more than one-third larger than the other. The equality of two variances is tested by computing the ratio of the two variances, and this ratio follows the F-distribution.

The formal assumption does not state that the two sample variances are equal, but that the variances are equal in the populations from which the two sets of observations came. If the assumption of equal population variances is true, then we should use all the data to estimate this common variance. This is a better use of the data than we made above, where we used part of the data to find the estimates s_1^2 and another part of the data to find the other estimates s_2^2.

One way to find a single, common estimate of the variance is to compute the mean of the two existing estimates; that is,

$$s^2 = (1/2)s_1^2 + (1/2)s_2^2$$

A difficulty with this way of combining the two estimates is that when the two groups do not have the same number of observations, the variance from the group with the larger number of observations is a better quantity, in some sense, and should therefore contribute more to the overall s^2 than the variance from the smaller group. The formula above does not allow for this, however, because it uses ½ as weights for both variances. It is better to use weights that involve the number of observations in each group, and the overall variance is usually found from the expression

$$s^2 = \frac{n_1 - 1}{n_1 + n_2 - 2} s_1^2 + \frac{n_2 - 1}{n_1 + n_2 - 2} s_2^2$$

$$= (4/8)10.00 + (4/8)6.50 = 8.25 \qquad s = 2.87$$

When the number of observations in the two groups is equal, this formula reduces to the first formula with ½ as weights. When the groups have different numbers of observations, the second formula gives more weight to the variance based on the larger number of observations.

Using the common s^2 the denominator for the t-statistic for the difference between two means becomes

$$\sqrt{s^2/n_1 + s^2/n_2} = s\sqrt{1/n_1 + 1/n_2}$$

The t-value itself is found as

$$t = \frac{\bar{y}_1 - \bar{y}_2}{s\sqrt{1/n_1 + 1/n_2}} = \frac{4 - 6}{2.87\sqrt{1/5 + 1/5}} = -1.10 \qquad 8 \text{ df}$$

which, in this particular case with the same number of observations in the two groups, is the same t-value as presented earlier. Instead of first finding the average variance s^2, the following equivalent formula works equally well,

$$t = \frac{\bar{y}_1 - \bar{y}_2}{\sqrt{s_1^2/n_2 + s_2^2/n_1}}$$

In this denominator the variance from the first group is divided by the number of observations in the second group, and vice versa.

Analysis of variance for two groups. The statistical analysis outlined above is the simplest example of an analysis of variance, even though it is usually not thought of a such. But the formula for t can be changed to become an F-ratio as used in analysis of variance. Below we show how this change is done in order to show the connection between the t-test for the equality of two means and analysis of variance.

First it can be noted that except for not being able to tell whether the sign of t is positive or negative, no other information is lost by squaring the t-value. Let us first work with the case where the two groups have the same number of observations on the dependent variable Y, that is, $n_1 = n_2 = n$. Then,

$$t^2 = \frac{(\bar{y}_1 - \bar{y}_2)^2}{s^2(1/n_1 + 1/n_2)} = \frac{n(\bar{y}_1 - \bar{y}_2)^2}{2s^2} = \frac{5(4-6)^2}{2(8.25)} = 1.21$$

tells us just as much as t itself, except whether the difference between the two means is positive or negative. But if the null hypothesis is a two-sided hypothesis, the sign does not matter anyway, since the alternative hypothesis only states that the two population means are different.

It is possible to rewrite the numerator for t^2. It can be shown that the difference between the two means can be written as the sum of two differences where each of the new differences is a difference between a group mean and the overall mean $\bar{y}$. Thus

$$(4-6)^2$$
$$= (\bar{y}_1 - \bar{y}_2)^2 = 2(\bar{y}_1 - \bar{y})^2 + 2(\bar{y}_2 - \bar{y})^2$$
$$= 2(4-5)^2 + 2(6-5)^2$$

Then we can rewrite the expression for t^2 the following way,

$$t^2 = \frac{n(\bar{y}_1 - \bar{y})^2 + n(\bar{y}_2 - \bar{y})^2}{s^2} = \frac{5(4-5)^2 + 5(6-5)^2}{8.25}$$

$$= 1.21$$

In the terminology of analysis of variance this quantity is called F with 1 and $2n - 2$ ($=8$) degrees of freedom. The numerator measures how much the group means differ from the overall mean. The denominator, which is the common variance in each of the groups, measures how much the observations are spread out around the group means. The same formula also applies when the number of observations in the two groups are not equal. When there are n_1 observations in the first group and n_2 in the second group, we get

$$F = \frac{n_1(\bar{y}_1 - \bar{y})^2 + n_2(\bar{y}_2 - \bar{y})^2}{s^2} \qquad \begin{array}{l} 1 \text{ and } n_1 + n_2 - 2 \\ \text{degrees of freedom} \end{array}$$

Now it is possible to return to graphs B and C in Figure 1 and see what we achieved. The numerator for the F-ratio will be the same for the two cases since the two group means $\bar{y}_1$ and $\bar{y}_2$ deviate from the overall mean $\bar{y}$ by the same magnitudes. But the denominator s^2 will differ; it will be large for case B and small for case C. In case B the observations are quite far from the mean in each of the two groups, and the variance s^2 (=8.25) will therefore be large. This again means that the F-value (=1.21) will be small.

In case C the situation is different. The observations are quite clustered around their group means, and the variance s^2 (=0.50) is therefore small. The value of F (=20.00) is large. The conclusion is that a large value of F tells us we have a significant difference between the two group means. From the t-table we recall that a value larger than 2 or smaller than –2 is usually significant. This means that with 2 groups, an F-value larger than 4 is similarly significant, since F is the square of t. In this example with 2 groups and 10 observations, we find from tables of the F-distribution that we need an F-value larger than 5.32 in order to call the observed difference $\bar{y}_1 - \bar{y}_2$ significant with a 5% significance level. With more than two groups and with many observations, F-values can be significant when they are as small as 2 or 3.

The value of F is approximately equal to 1.00 where there is no difference between the population means and the difference between the sample means is due only to random fluctuations. The reason for that is as follows. When we have a sample of n observations of a random variable with variance s^2, we can find the variance of the sample mean $(s_{\bar{y}}^2)$ from the equation

$$s_{\bar{y}}^2 = s^2/n$$

Using the data from case B, we have $s^2 = 8.25$ and n = 5, which gives

$$s_{\bar{y}}^2 = 8.25/5 = 1.65$$

The interpretation of this variance is that if we had a large number of samples of 5 observations from the same population and computed the mean from each sample, then the variance of these sample means would be approximately equal to 1.65.

We are not in the situation here of having many samples, but we do have two samples and thereby two means $\overline{y}_1$ and $\overline{y}_2$, and we can find the variance of these two means using the ordinary formula for a variance. Thus another estimate of the variance of the means becomes

$$s_{\overline{y}}^2 = \{(\overline{y}_1 - \overline{y})^2 + (\overline{y}_2 - \overline{y})^2\}/(2-1)$$
$$= \{(4-5)^2 + (6-5)^2\}/1 = 2.00$$

If the differences in the sample means are due only to random fluctuations, then these two estimates 1.65 and 2.00 should be about equal. One way to find out how equal they are is to take their ratio, which should be about equal to 1.00. Here

$$F = 2.00/1.65 = 1.21$$

which is the same F-value we had above for these data. Since the ratio is so close to 1.00, we conclude that the difference between the two means is only due to random fluctuations, and the population means are not different.

In case C the situation is different. There the F-ratio equals 20.00, and about the only reason it is that large is that the difference between the two means is due to something more than random fluctuations. Thus there is every reason to believe that the two groups of observations are two samples that do not come from populations with equal means.

The computations necessary for an analysis of variance as it has been performed above are usually summarized in a table like Table 2, which shows the data from case B. The numbers on the first line of the table refer to the group means. The difference between the group means is measured by the sum of squares.

$$n_1(\overline{y}_1 - \overline{y})^2 + n_2(\overline{y}_2 - \overline{y})^2 = 5(4-5)^2 + 5(6-5)^2 = 10.00$$

This sum is sometimes called the between group sum of squares or simply the group sum of squares.

This sum is found from the two terms $\overline{y}_1 - \overline{y}$ and $\overline{y}_2 - \overline{y}$; and if we are told the value of one of these terms, then we automatically know the value of the other term. Another way of saying the same thing is that the between-group sum of squares is based on one degree of freedom when we have two groups. By dividing a sum of squares by its degrees of freedom, we get what is called the corresponding mean square. Here the between-group mean square becomes $10.00/1 = 10.00$.

The next entry in Table 2 is the F-ratio, measuring whether or not there is a systematic difference between the group means. The last entry on the first line gives the probability of observing an F-value as large as the one we got or larger, under the assumption that the population means are equal. If the population means are equal, we know that F is approximately equal to 1.00. If the population means are equal, the probability is 0.30 that F is larger than or equal to the observed value 1.21. This probability is quite large, and there is therefore nothing unusual about an F-value of this magnitude. But when the probability is less than 0.05, or 0.01, or whatever significance level we choose, we conclude that the assumption of equal population means must be wrong. In that case the difference between the sample means is significant, and the population means are therefore different. But a small probability only helps us establish that the population means are different; it says nothing about whether the difference is large or small. Usually, only large differences are of any substantive interest.

The numbers on the second line in Table 2 refer to the variation in the observations within the two groups, leading to the common estimate s^2 of the variance within the groups. We have seen above that the numerator for s^2 measures how much the observations differ from their group means. When we add up the deviations of the observations from their respective means, we get the sum of squares

$$(y_{11} - \overline{y}_1)^2 + (y_{12} - \overline{y}_1)^2 + \ldots + (y_{15} - \overline{y}_1)^2$$
$$+ (y_{21} - \overline{y}_2)^2 + (y_{22} - \overline{y}_2)^2 + \ldots + (y_{25} - \overline{y}_2)^2$$
$$= (9 - 4)^2 + (5 - 4)^2 + (3 - 4)^2 + (2 - 4)^2 + (1 - 4)^2$$
$$+ (8 - 6)^2 + (8 - 6)^2 + (7 - 6)^2 + (5 - 6)^2 + (2 - 6)^2 = 66.00$$

Since the sum of squared deviations in each group is based on $n-1 = 4$ degrees of freedom and there are two groups, this sum of squares has 8 degrees of freedom. The common variance of the dependent variable Y in each of the two groups is obtained by dividing the within-group sum of squares by its degrees of freedom, thereby giving us the within-group

TABLE 2
Analysis of Variance Table for the Data in Case B

Source	Sum of Squares	Degrees of Freedom	Mean Square	F-ratio	Significance
Between	10.00	1	10.00	1.21	0.30
Within groups	66.00	8	8.25		
Total	76.00	9			

mean square of $66.00/8 = 8.25$. Finally, the F-value is obtained by dividing the two mean squares.

The last line in the table, marked total, is obtained by adding the sums of squares and degrees of freedom. These numbers do not have much use in the analysis, even though it is sometimes easier to find the within-group sum of squares as the difference between the total sum of squares and the between-group sum of squares rather than directly, as we did above. The total sum of squares is obtained by subtracting the overall mean from each of the observations, squaring all these differences and adding them. The overall mean in the example is 5, and the total variation of the observations around this mean becomes

$$(y_{11} - \bar{y})^2 + (y_{12} - \bar{y})^2 + \ldots + (y_{15} - \bar{y})^2$$
$$+ (y_{21} - \bar{y})^2 + (y_{22} - \bar{y})^2 + \ldots + (y_{25} - \bar{y})^2$$
$$= (9 - 5)^2 + (5 - 5)^2 + (3 - 5)^2 + (2 - 5)^2 + (1 - 5)^2$$
$$+ (8 - 5)^2 + (8 - 5)^2 + (7 - 5)^2 + (5 - 5)^2 + (2 - 5)^2 = 76.00$$

With 10 observations this sum has 9 degrees of freedom.

Statistical theory. There is a formal mathematical theory that underlies the analysis we have done above; and while we do not present the full theory here, it is important to realize some aspects of that theory. Part of the theory is presented here, and another part is presented at the end of this chapter.

The analysis is founded on the assumption that we can decompose each observed value of the dependent variable into three additive terms; that is, we have to be able to write each observation as a sum of three terms. The decomposition can be written observation = overall mean

+ deviation of group mean from overall mean

+ deviation of observation from group mean

The overall mean is a constant, common to all the observations. The deviation of a group mean from the overall mean is taken to represent the effect on each observation of belonging to that particular group. In our example, the effect of belonging to the first group is $\bar{y}_1 - \bar{y} = 4 - 5 = -1$, and the effect of belonging to the second group is measured as $\bar{y}_2 - \bar{y} = 6 - 5 = 1$. Thus part of the reason the observed values are what they are is that for each person in the first group a one has been subtracted from the overall mean, and for each person in the second group a one has been added to the overall mean. The -1 is the effect of being in the control group, and the $+1$ is the effect of being in the experimental group.

Finally, the difference between an observation and the mean for the group is taken to represent the effect of all other variables. These terms are also called the residuals. For the data in case C the residuals are

$$-1, 0, 0, 0, 1 \quad \text{and} \quad -1, 0, 0, 0, 1$$

Since each set of residuals is deviations from group means, it is not surprising that they add up to zero in each group. The sum of the squared residuals equals 4.00, and this is the sum we also have called the within sum of squares.

For the 10 observations in case C we get the following decompositions:

$$
\begin{array}{lll}
3 = 5 - 1 - 1 & \text{and} & 5 = 5 + 1 - 1 \\
4 = 5 - 1 + 0 & & 6 = 5 + 1 + 0 \\
4 = 5 - 1 + 0 & & 6 = 5 + 1 + 0 \\
4 = 5 - 1 + 0 & & 6 = 5 + 1 + 0 \\
5 = 5 - 1 + 1 & & 7 = 5 + 1 + 1
\end{array}
$$

The general expression becomes

$$y_{ij} = \bar{y} + (\bar{y}_i - \bar{y}) + (\bar{y}_{ij} - \bar{y}_i)$$

where i equals 1 or 2 and refers to the two groups, while j equals 1, 2, 3, 4, or 5 and refers to the observations within each group.

Use of the F-test requires the residuals to have a normal distribution. The histogram of the 10 residuals for the data in case C is shown in Figure 2. While we do not have a normal distribution in that figure, we do have a unimodal, bell-shaped histogram, satisfactorily indicating that we may well have an underlying normal distribution of the residuals for the entire population.

The residuals will not always display a distribution that follows a normal distribution as closely as the distribution shown in Figure 2. With only moderate departures from normality, experience has shown that the statistical tests discussed here are not affected. Another way of saying the same thing is to say that t-tests and F-tests are robust tests. When the departure from normality is more severe, it may be possible to change the original observations of the dependent variable and thereby make the distribution of the residuals more like a normal distribution.

Such transformations of the observations can be used to make heavily skewed distributions more symmetric. For example, a skewed distribution with many small and few large observations will become more symmetric if we use the square root of each observation in the analysis rather than the original values. Other types of distributions may be more problematic. A u-shaped distribution, for example, cannot be changed into a bell-shaped distribution by any meaningful transformation. In such cases it is still possible to make the computations of all the sums of squares and mean squares, but one must be much more careful in one's interpretation of the significance level used in the test. The distribution of the residuals is discussed further in Chapter 3 in the section on the residual variable.

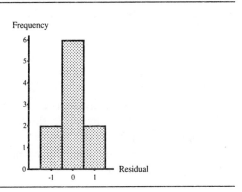

Figure 2: Histogram of Residuals for Data in Case C

There is a major complication with what we have done so far. The differences $\bar{y}_1 - \bar{y}$ and $\bar{y}_2 - \bar{y}$ are only estimates of the true effects on the dependent variable of belonging to the control and experimental groups. Similarly, the residuals are only estimates of the effects of all other variables. Finally, $\bar{y}$ is only an estimate of the overall level of the dependent variable.

The formal model, which specifies an additive model involving the true effects, can be written

$$y_{ij} = \mu + \alpha_i + \epsilon_{ij}$$

As before, i refers to the group, and j refers to the observation within the group. In this model μ is a constant and refers to the overall level of the dependent variable; α_1 and α_2 represent the effect on an observation of being in groups 1 and 2, respectively. The ϵ_{ij} is the effect on the j-th observation in the i-th group of all other variables, and in our example we have 10 such terms: $\epsilon_{11}, \epsilon_{12}, \epsilon_{13}, \epsilon_{14}, \epsilon_{15}, \epsilon_{21}, \epsilon_{22}, \epsilon_{23}, \epsilon_{24}$ and ϵ_{25}. These 10 residual terms are assumed to come from a normal distribution with mean zero and variance σ^2.

Instead of knowing μ, the 2 α's, and the 10 ϵ's, we have 10 observations (the y's) located in two groups. The observations are used to find estimates of the true, unknown effects designated by Greek letters. We can never verify whether the true effects are additive and whether the true residuals have a normal distribution. But we can look at the distribution of the estimated residuals and hope that if this distribution looks fairly normal, then the distribution of the true residuals is not too far from normal. Thus one should always find the estimated residuals and examine their distribution for normality.

More Than Two Groups

Analysis of variance. We can now turn to the case in which the independent variable has more than two categories. If the independent variable is political affiliation, we may have Democrat, Republican, independent, other parties, and apolitical as the categories. With religious affiliation we may have Catholic, Jew, Protestant, other, and none. Each category determines a group of observations of the dependent variable, and in the general case we have k groups rather than two.

The economy, of course, is a book with many chapters, and economic issues come in many versions. Most analyses of economic voting zero in on such indicators as unemployment, inflation, the federal deficit, and foreign trade. Do the mass media affect the salience of each of those four economic issues equally? To answer this question we expand the experimental condition to include four treatments. The control group again will be shown an economy-less newscast, treatment group A will be shown the same newscast plus a story on unemployment; group B one on inflation instead; group C one on the deficit; and group D one on foreign trade. Five subjects will be randomly assigned to each of the five conditions and afterwards asked to fill out a questionnaire in which they are querried, among other things, about the importance of the state of the economy.

The dependent variable is the same as earlier, an evaluation of the importance of the economy on a ten-point scale. Our concern is with whether the five groups differ on this variable, where the groups are thought to be different if their means are different. If the five sample means are not all equal, then we have a relationship between type of newscast and people's view of the economy in the sample. Often, we are more interested in whether the means are equal or not in the corresponding five populations than whether simply the sample means differ.

As before, we have to investigate whether the differences in the sample means are random variations that occurred just by chance or whether there are systematic differences between the means. We have to go through the same type of reasoning we did with two groups and compare the variation in the means with how much the observations vary within each of the groups. The five group means are shown in Table 3, and the observations themselves are shown as points in the scatterplot in Figure 3.

TABLE 3
Evaluation of Economy: Observations and Means by Groups

Group	Observations	Mean
A Unemployment story	6 6 6 8 9	7.0
B Inflation story	7 8 8 8 9	8.0
C Deficit story	4 4 5 6 6	5.0
D Foreign trade story	5 5 6 6 8	6.0
E No economic story	3 4 4 4 5	4.0
		Overall mean 6.0

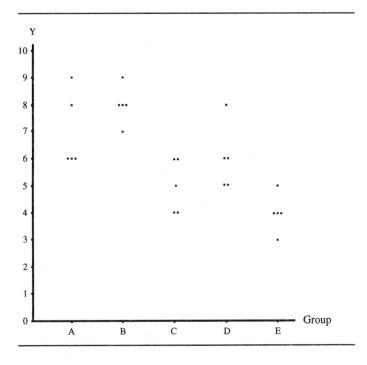

Figure 3: Scatterplot of Data in Table 3

For the sake of simplicity and without any loss of generality, we restrict ourselves in this example to a small number of cases in each group. The numerical values are hypothetical and constructed to be easy to work with. In this example all groups have the same number of observations; but for an analysis of variance as it is done here, it makes little or no difference whether the numbers of observations are the same or not.

The analysis proceeds as follows. The 25 observations have different values, and one way to measure how different they are is to subtract the overall mean $\overline{y} = 6.0$ from each observation, square all the differences, and add the squares. This gives the total sum of squares, TSS, where

$$TSS = \Sigma(y_{ij} - \overline{y})^2$$
$$= (6 - 6.0)^2 + (6 - 6.0)^2 + (6 - 6.0)^2 + (8 - 6.0)^2 + (9 - 6.0)^2$$
$$+ (7 - 6.0)^2 + (7 - 6.0)^2 + (7 - 6.0)^2 + (8 - 6.0)^2 + (9 - 6.0)^2$$
$$+ (4 - 6.0)^2 + (4 - 6.0)^2 + (5 - 6.0)^2 + (6 - 6.0)^2 + (6 - 6.0)^2$$

$$+ (5 - 6.0)^2 + (5 - 6.0)^2 + (6 - 6.0)^2 + (6 - 6.0)^2 + (8 - 6.0)^2$$
$$+ (3 - 6.0)^2 + (4 - 6.0)^2 + (4 - 6.0)^2 + (4 - 6.0)^2 + (5 - 6.0)^2$$
$$= 72.0$$

There is a simpler and more accurate way to compute this sum, namely

$$\text{TSS} = \Sigma y_{ij}^2 - (\Sigma y_{ij})^2 / n$$
$$= (6^2 + 6^2 + \ldots + 5^2) - (6 + 6 + \ldots + 5)^2 / 25$$
$$= 972 - 150^2 / 25 = 72.0$$

With this formula it is not necessary to subtract the mean from every term before squaring. Instead, the formula requires the sum of the squared observations minus the squared sum of the observations themselves divided by the total number of observations.

There is another way to think about this total sum of squares. A particular observed value of the economic importance variable has the value it does for two reasons. One reason is that the value is affected by which of the groups the person belongs to, that is, which newscast the person viewed. The other reason is that the person's value is affected by a whole set of other variables, for example, age, education, occupation, etc. The net effect of all these variables is what we call the residual variable. Thus a particular observation is determined by the group and the residual variable. Suppose, for a moment, that neither one of these two had any effect. Then every person would have the same, identical value of the economic importance variable. There would be nothing affecting this variable; and no matter how different people are on other variables, they would have the same value on the economic importance variable.

The best estimate of this common value would be the overall mean 6.0. The degree to which each of the observed values is different from 6.0 then becomes a measure of the combined effect of the group variable and the residual variable. One way to measure how large this effect is to find how different each observation is from 6.0. Next, by squaring each difference and adding the squares, we get a measurement of how large the combined effect is of the group variable and the residual variable. Thus, in this example the combined effect of the type of newscast and the residual variable equals 72.0. An obvious next step is to try to break this combined effect into separate effects for the type of newscast and the residual variable, and that is done below.

The degrees of freedom for this total sum of squares becomes 24. In the general case the degrees of freedom for the total sum of squares equal the total number of observations minus one. There are 25 terms in the total sum of squares here, and having 24 degrees of freedom means we need to know only 24 of the values in order to find all 25. If we know that the first 24 values are

$$0.0 \quad 0.0 \quad 0.0 \quad 2.0 \quad 3.0 \ldots -2.0 \quad -2.0$$

then we know from these values that the twenty-fifth value has to equal −1.0. This is because the sum of all 25 values equals zero, and the sum of the first 24 equals 1.0. Thus the last value has to equal −1.0. The reason why the numbers add to zero is that they are deviations from their overall mean.

Because the last value was "hidden" in the previous 24, that value does not contain any new information beyond what we already knew from the first 24 values. Therefore, even though the total sum of squares TSS is computed from a sum of 25 squared numbers, the total information in these numbers is contained in the first 24, and we express this by saying that TSS has 24 degrees of freedom.

The extent to which the means in the groups are different is measured by the between-group sum of squares, BSS. This sum is found by taking the difference between each group mean $\bar{y}_i$ and the overall mean $\bar{y}$, squaring each difference, multiplying the square by the number of observations in the group n_i, and adding these products. This is the same computation we made with two groups. Here we get

$$
\begin{aligned}
\text{BSS} &= \Sigma n_i (\bar{y}_i - \bar{y})^2 \\
&= 5(7.0 - 6.0)^2 + 5(8.0 - 6.0)^2 + 5(5.0 - 6.0)^2 \\
&\quad + 5(6.0 - 6.0)^2 + 5(4.0 - 6.0)^2 \\
&= 50.0
\end{aligned}
$$

This sum has 4 degrees of freedom. There are 5 terms in the sum, but we can find the fifth difference if we know the first 4. In the general case the number of degrees of freedom for the between group sum of squares equals one less than the number of groups.

The between group sum of squares, or simply the group sum of squares, measures how large the effect is of the group variable. In this example 50.0 measures the effect of the different newscasts on the evaluation-of-the-economy variable. Suppose for a moment that type of newscast had no effect. Then the mean of the dependent variable would be the same in all the groups, and they would all equal the overall mean 6.0. But these means are not equal, since type of newscast does have an effect on these individuals. One way to measure that effect for each person is to find the difference between the mean of the group the person belongs to and the overall mean. For exmple, the effect of being in the control groups becomes $\bar{y}_5 - \bar{y} = 4.0 - 6.0 = -2.0$ for each person in that group, and similarly for the people in the other groups. The overall magnitude of these effects can be found by squaring this difference for each person and adding up the squares. Since each person in the fifth group has the effect $(-2.0)^2$, we can multiply this square by five rather than adding it up five times. Doing this for all 25 observation gives a combined effect of 50.0 for the type of newscast.

In addition to being in different groups, the observations are different because people are affected by the residual variable in different ways. Now we need to measure the effect of the residual variable. So far, we have found that the combined effect of type of newscast and the residual variable equals 72.0. Also, the effect of type of newscast alone equals 50.0. This leads us to assigning the difference between the two sums of squares, $72.0 - 50.0 = 22.0$, as the effect of the residual variable. Since there are 24 degrees of freedom for the total sum of squares and 4 degrees of freedom for the sum of squares for type of newscast, 20 degrees of freedom are for the residual sum of squares.

There is another way of thinking about the effect of the residual variable. Suppose the residual variable had no effect. Then all the observations in the control group would be the same, since the only effect on those people is that they are in the control group. Similarly for the other groups, within each group the observed values of the dependent variable would be the same. The best estimate of the common value in each group would be the observed mean in that group. In the control group all the observations would be 4.0, in group A they would be 7.0, and so on. But these are not the values we observed, because the residual variable does have an effect. The difference between an observed value and the group mean therefore has to be the effect of the residual variable for that person. For each person we can find the effect of the residual variable; and if we square these effects and add the squares, we find the overall effect of the residual variable.

All 25 residuals are shown in Table 4. The table also shows the sum of squared residuals in each group and the overall residual sum of squares, which is equal to 22.0. This is the same sum we found above as the

TABLE 4
Residuals Arranged by Group, Their Sum of Squares
and Degrees of Freedom

Group	Residuals					Sum of Squares	Degrees of Freedom
A	−1.0	−1.0	−1.0	1.0	2.0	8.0	4
B	−1.0	0.0	0.0	0.0	1.0	2.0	4
C	−1.0	−1.0	0.0	1.0	1.0	4.0	4
D	−1.0	−1.0	0.0	0.0	2.0	6.0	4
E	−1.0	0.0	0.0	0.0	1.0	2.0	4
					Residual sum of squares	22.0	20

difference between the total sum of squares and the sum of squares for the type of newscast.

As for degrees of freedom, the residuals add to zero in each group. Thus, if there are n_i observations in the i-th group, the sum of squared residuals in that group have $n_i - 1$ degrees of freedom. In our case, with 5 observations in each group, there are 4 degrees of freedom in each group. Added across all the group, we get 20 degrees of freedom for the residual sum of squares. In the general case the degrees of freedom for the residual sum of squares equal the total number of observations minus the number of groups.

The sums of squares and degrees of freedom we have found are displayed in an analysis of variance table in Table 5. Also, in that table the group and residual sums of squares are divided by their degrees of freedom to get the corresponding mean squares. The group mean square equals 12.5, and the residual mean square equals 1.1. The residual mean square is another name for the estimate of the common variance of the residuals. Since the variance equals 1.1, the standard deviation of the residuals equals the square root, or 1.05. One way to interpret this standard deviation is to say that the average deviation of the observations from their group means, that is, the average residual, equals 1.05. Looking at the magnitudes of the 25 residuals in Table 4, that seems like a reasonable average.

As before, we are usually not as interested in whether the observed sample group means are different as we are in the question of whether the means in the populations from which the samples came are different. The null hypothesis states that the population means are equal, and the hypothesis is tested by the F-ratio. The F is found as the ratio of the

TABLE 5
Analysis of Variance Table for the Data in Figure 3

Source	Sum of Squares	Degrees of Freedom	Mean Square	F-ratio	Significance
Groups	50.0	4	12.5	11.36	0.00006
Residual	22.0	20	1.1		
Total	72.0	24			
$E^2 = 0.65$					

group mean square to the residual mean square, and in the example F = 12.5/1.1 = 11.36. Again, a value around 1.00 tells us that the differences in the group means is only a random variation from sample to sample. When the F-ratio is a good deal larger than 1.00, we can conclude that the variation in the group means is more than what could have been expected by chance alone, and the population means are therefore different.

From a table of the F distribution we find that with 4 and 20 degrees of freedom, we need a value of F larger than 2.87 in order to reject the null hypothesis with a 5% significance level. With a smaller, 1% significance level, F has to be larger than 4.43. Since our observed value of F is larger than either of these cutoffs, the null hypothesis of equal population means is rejected. Indeed it is possible to find that if the population means are really equal, the probability of observing F equal to or larger than our value 11.36 is only 0.00006. Since this probability is so small, we have strong evidence for the notion that the population means are different.

This immediately raises the next question: How different are the population means? To get some idea of the magnitudes of the differences, we take the sample means as estimates of the corresponding population means. That way, the differences between the sample means become estimates of the differences between the population means. One way to study these differences in more detail is to put confidence intervals around the sample means and examine the evidence in these intervals. Such multiple comparisons of the sample means are commonly discussed in more extensive presentations of analysis of variance.

The residuals should be examined for any unusual patterns like single extreme values and the extent to which they follow a normal distribution. A histogram of the 25 residuals is drawn in Figure 4, and it shows a variable with a mean of zero and a unimodal distribution. In this case

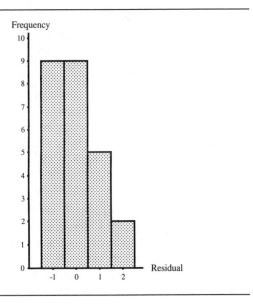

Figure 4: Histogram of Residuals in Table 4

the distribution is somewhat skewed. The distribution of the residuals is discussed further in Chapter 3 in the section on the residual variable.

The correlation ratio. The effect of the newscast variable on the economic variable can be measured in two different ways. The effect of a particular type of newscast on the economic variable can be measured as the difference between the mean for that newscast and the overall mean. The overall effect of all the newscasts, moreover, can be measured by the group (between) sum of squares. But we do not have yet any measure of the relationship between the explanatory and the dependent variable that resembles a correlation coefficient, giving the strength of the relationship between the two variables.

One way to get such a measure is as follows. If we had all the values of Y and were asked to estimate the value for a particular individual, one possible estimate would be the overall mean $\bar{y}$. This is a value located in the middle of the observations; and in the absence of any information about the individual, it seems reasonable to choose such a central value as our estimate. If the true value equals y_{ij}, then the error we make in the estimation becomes the difference $y_{ij} - \bar{y}$. Suppose the "penalty" we have to suffer for this error is the square of the error, that is $(y_{ij} - \bar{y})^2$. If we did this for all the respondents and used the mean as an estimate each time, then the total "penalty" would be the sum of all the squared errors, $\Sigma(y_{ij}$

$-y)^2$. This is the total sum of squares in analysis of variance. For the data in our example this number equals 72.0.

Next, change the guessing game in such a way that we are now told what group an observation belongs to. Our best predicted value of Y would then be the mean in that group, $\overline{y}_i$. The error we now make becomes the difference between the true value y_{ij} and this predicted value. The "penalty" is still the square of the error, that is, $(y_{ij} - \overline{y}_i)^2$. The overall "penalty" for doing this for all the observations then becomes the sum of these squares. This is the residual sum of squares as we know it from analysis of variance. In our example the sum equals 22.0, as a measure of how well we can predict the economic scores from knowing which of the groups the people belong to.

Knowing the group improves our ability to predict. There is a reduction in the "penalty" from 72.0 to 22.0 when we are told about the group membership. The improvement in prediction becomes the difference between these two sums of squares, or 50.0. In itself this number does not tell us much, and it is more informative if we compute the relative improvement,

$$E^2 = (72.0 - 22.0)/72.0 = (TSS - RSS)/TSS$$
$$= 0.69$$

Thus there is a 69% improvement in our ability to predict the values of the dependent variable when we know what group an observation belongs to. This quantity is called the correlation ratio and is sometimes denoted as eta squared. It is the ratio of the between group sum of squares to the total sum of squares. It tells us how much of the variation in the dependent variable is explained by the explanatory variable, in the sense of how much our prediction is improved by knowing the group when the "penalty" is measured by the square of the prediction error.

The same quantity is also computed in regression analysis and is there denoted R^2, where R is the multiple correlation coefficient.

Formal model. It is now possible to return in somewhat greater detail to the formal model for what is called a fixed effect one-way analysis of variance. The model specifies that an observed value of the dependent variable Y can be written as a sum of three components. That is, we believe that the substantive process that generated the observed data can be expressed in the equation

Observation

= constant

> \+ effect of being in a particular group
> (effect of the independent variable X)
>
> \+ residual

This is a model of the real world, and it can be translated into mathematical symbols. For the j-th observation in the i-th group, we can write the model in the equation

$$y_{ij} = \mu + \alpha_i + \epsilon_{ij}$$

where μ is the constant, α_i is the effect of being in group i, and ϵ_{ij} is the effect of the residual variable, which is the net effect of all other variables, including measurement errors.

As usual with a statistical model of this kind, we want to find estimates of the parameters and thereby investigate the effect of the explanatory variable on the dependent variable, and we want to see how well the data fit the model.

First, we have to realize that the equation above is a very compact way of expressing this model. There is an equation like this for every observation, and in our example we have the following 25 equations:

$$y_{11} = \mu + \alpha_1 \qquad\qquad + \epsilon_{11}$$

$$\cdot \quad \cdot \quad \cdot \qquad \text{(group 1)} \qquad \cdot$$

$$\cdot \quad \cdot \quad \cdot \qquad\qquad\qquad \cdot$$

$$y_{15} = \mu + \alpha_1 \qquad\qquad + \epsilon_{15}$$

$$y_{21} = \mu \qquad + \alpha_2 \qquad\qquad + \epsilon_{21}$$

$$\cdot \quad \cdot \quad \cdot \qquad \text{(group 2)} \qquad \cdot$$

$$\cdot \quad \cdot \quad \cdot \qquad\qquad\qquad \cdot$$

$$y_{25} = \mu \qquad + \alpha_2 \qquad\qquad + \epsilon_{25}$$

$$y_{31} = \mu \qquad\qquad + \alpha_3 \qquad + \epsilon_{31}$$

$$\cdot \quad \cdot \quad \cdot \qquad \text{(group 3)} \qquad \cdot$$

$$\cdot \quad \cdot \quad \cdot \qquad\qquad\qquad \cdot$$

$$y_{35} = \mu \qquad\qquad + \alpha_3 \qquad + \epsilon_{35}$$

$$y_{41} = \mu \qquad\qquad\qquad + \alpha_4 \qquad + \epsilon_{41}$$

$$\cdot \quad \cdot \quad \cdot \qquad \text{(group 4)} \qquad \cdot$$

$$\cdot \quad \cdot \quad \cdot \qquad\qquad\qquad \cdot$$

$$y_{45} = \mu \qquad\qquad + \alpha_4 \qquad + \epsilon_{45}$$
$$y_{51} = \mu \qquad\qquad\quad + \alpha_5 + \epsilon_{51}$$
$$\cdot \qquad \cdot \qquad \cdot \qquad\quad \text{(group 5)} \qquad \cdot$$
$$\cdot \qquad \cdot \qquad \cdot$$
$$y_{55} = \mu \qquad\qquad\quad + \alpha_5 + \epsilon_{55}$$
$$25 \text{ df} = 1 \text{ df} \qquad + 4 \text{ df} \qquad + 20 \text{ df}$$

There are 25 terms on the left side of these equations, and they have a total of 25 degrees of freedom since there are no restrictions on these numbers. On the right side there is one μ, which then has one degree of freedom. There are five α's; but their sum equals zero, and they therefore have four degrees of freedom. There are 25 ϵ's; but since on the average their mean is zero in every group, they have only 20 degrees of freedom. The μ and the α's are the parameters of the model, and the ϵ's measure how well the model fits. Figure 5 gives a graphic representation of the model showing how the observed value of Y is decomposed into the three parts.

The first task is to find numerical estimates of the parameters in the model. We have 25 equations in the example above, and only the Y values are known. But the equations cannot be solved directly for the unknowns. Instead, we use the method of least squares to find estimated numerical values for the unknown. This method uses as estimates the values of the parameters that make the sum of the squared residuals

$$\Sigma \, \epsilon_{ij}^2 = \Sigma (y_{ij} - \mu - \alpha_i)^2$$

as small as possible. The estimates are denoted by Greek letters with a "^" above. The smallest sum of squares is obtained when

$$\hat{\mu} = \overline{y} \qquad \text{overall mean}$$
$$\hat{\alpha}_i = \overline{y}_i - \overline{y} \qquad \text{deviation of group mean from overall mean}$$

For our example we get the estimates

$$\hat{\mu} = \overline{y} = 6.0 \qquad \hat{\alpha}_1 = \overline{y}_1 - \overline{y} = 7.0 - 6.0 = 1.0$$
$$\hat{\alpha}_2 = \overline{y}_2 - \overline{y} = 8.0 - 6.0 = 2.0$$
$$\hat{\alpha}_3 = \overline{y}_3 - \overline{y} = 5.0 - 6.0 = -1.0$$
$$\hat{\alpha}_4 = \overline{y}_4 - \overline{y} = 6.0 - 6.0 = 0.0$$
$$\hat{\alpha}_5 = \overline{y}_5 - \overline{y} = 4.0 - 6.0 = -2.0$$

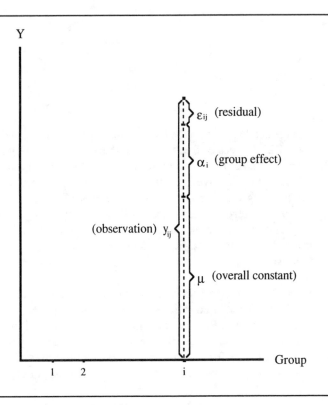

Figure 5: Decomposition of the j-th Observation in the i-th Group into Three Components

With these estimated parameters the estimated residuals are found from the expression

$$\hat{\varepsilon}_{ij} = y_{ij} - \overline{y}_i$$

The estimated residuals are listed above in Table 4. The sum of the squared residuals equals 22.0, and there is no way we can find other estimates of the parameters that will produce a smaller sum of squared residuals.

The statistical null hypothesis that the population group means are equal is equivalent to the statement that the α's are equal to zero, since they measure the differences between the groups. This hypothesis can be tested using the F-ratio, when the residuals have a normal distribution.

Let us look more closely at why the F-ratio can be used to test this null hypothesis. F is a fraction in which the numerator is the group (between) mean square, and the denominator is the residual (within) mean square. It is possible to show that the denominator is an estimate of the variance of the residuals, σ^2. In the more technical analysis of variance literature this is often expressed by saying that the expected value of the residual mean square equals σ^2. The numerator is more complicated, but it can be shown that it is an estimate of the quantity

$$\sigma^2 + (n_1\alpha_1^2 + n_2\alpha_2^2 + n_3\alpha_3^2 + n_4\alpha_4^2 + n_5\alpha_5^2)/4$$

This expression is known as the expected between group mean square. By dividing the expression for the numerator by the expression for the denominator of F, we get the ratio of the two expected mean squares. This ratio becomes

$$1.00 + (5\alpha_1^2 + 5\alpha_2^2 + 5\alpha_3^2 + 5\alpha_4^2 + 5\alpha_5^2)/4\sigma^2$$

Now there are two possibilities. Either the null hypothesis is true, which means that the α's are all equal to zero, or the null hypothesis is false and the α's are not all equal to zero. If the null hypothesis is true, then the expression above is equal to 1.00. On the other hand, if it is false, then the expression is larger than 1.00. Our observed value of F equals 9.19, which is either a bad estimate of 1.00 or an estimate of something larger than 1.00. Since F is as large as it is, we prefer to think that it is an estimate of something larger than 1.00, which is only possible if at least some of the alphas are different from zero. Thus we conclude that the null hypothesis is false.

Even when the null hypothesis is true, we do not get F-values that are exactly equal to 1.00. Our observed mean squares are only estimates, and they vary from sample to sample. This raises the question of what the cutoff values are for F such that the null hypothesis is not rejected for smaller observed values of F and rejected for values larger than the cutoff. The answers are found in the F-table, which provide us with the proper cutoff values.

Because any F is characterized by a pair of degrees of freedom, the number of groups minus one and the number of observations minus the number of groups, the F-tables are not as detailed as other tables. There is usually a separate table giving F-values for a 5% significance and another table for a 1% significance. The meaning of an entry in, say, the 5% table is that the probability equals only 0.05 of observing an F that large or larger under the condition that the null hypothesis is really true. Thus, when a null hypothesis is actually true, we only get an observed value of F larger than the value in the table 5% of the time across repeated samples. When a null hypothesis is actually false, we get large F-values much more often. Thus, when we observe a large value of F, we conclude that the null hypothesis must be false, even though it is also possible we might have gotten one of those unusual samples with a large F from populations where the group means are equal.

Computing and numerical results. Unless we have a small number of observations and few groups, the computations necessary for a one-way analysis of variance are better done on a computer. All standard statistical program packages have a program for such an analysis. The user only has to specify a few commands on how the data are organized in terms of the independent and the dependent variable and which output is wanted. One commonly used program package in the social sciences is SPSS-X, and it contains two relevant programs called ONEWAY and ANOVA. Analysis of variance programs are also found in the MINITAB package, which is particularly easy to use, and other possible packages are SAS, BMDP, and OSIRIS. Most statistical packages for microcomputers also have facilities for analysis of variance. This software is often much easier to use, even though the programs usually do not include as many options.

3. TWO-WAY ANALYSIS OF VARIANCE, ALL CATEGORIES

Unrelated Explanatory Variables

Introducing one more variable. The economy, like other things, may affect people differently depending on whether the news is good or bad. It has been argued that voters take prosperity for granted and feel no need to reward the incumbent government for what they consider the normal state of the economy. On the other hand, recessions or spurts of inflation lead to "throw the rascals out" reactions, with a negative electoral response being the result (Bloom and Price, 1975; Kernell, 1977; Lanoue, 1986). The assumption is that people only pay attention to the economy as an issue when things go bad. This question can be studied using an experiment with two explanatory variables, also known as factors.

TABLE 6
Allocations of Groups to Factors

Valence of Coverage	Economic Issue Covered in Newscast	
	Unemployment	Inflation
Positive	Group H	Group I
Negative	Group J	Group K

The first variable is the same as the one we used in Chapter 2: economic issues in the newscast. Let us focus on the two economic issues that have most preoccupied the public as well as governments in recent years: unemployment and inflation. Thus, in one type of newscast there is a story on unemployment and in the other type there is a story on inflation. The second, new variable refers to whether the economic news is good or bad: the valence of the coverage, in other words. This variable also has two categories; in one type of newscast the news is positive and in the other the news is negative.

These two variables together define four different experimental conditions, as shown in Table 6. Each condition is used for a separate sample of respondents. All four groups of respondents are shown essentially the same newscast, except for the following modifications. The newscast shown to group H includes a story with good news on unemployment, and the newscast for group I contains a story with good news on inflation. Similarly, the newscast for group J contains a story with bad news about unemployment, and group K gets a story with bad news about inflation. This covers all possible combinations of the two factors, and this plan is an example of what is known as a factorial design.

A total of 12 subjects are randomly allocated to the various experimental conditions in such a way that the same number of subjects sees a particular newscast. That way 3 subjects see each type of newscast. It is an important part of the design of this experiment that the number of subjects is the same for various conditions. We return to this issue below in the section on relationship between explanatory variables.

After watching their respective newscasts, the subjects are asked about the importance of the economy as an issue, using the same ten-point scale as before. The observed values of this dependent variable are shown in Table 7, together with the means in each of the cells in the

TABLE 7
Rating Scores and Means of the Importance of
the Economy, by Issue and Valence

Valence of Coverage	Economic Issue Covered in Newscast				Mean
	Unemployment		Inflation		
Positive	1 2 3	(2.0)	5 6 7	(6.0)	4.0
Negative	7 8 9	(8.0)	7 7 10	(8.0)	8.0
Mean	5.0		7.0		6.0

table and the means for the rows and columns. By reading across the rows of this table, we can sense the differences in the rating of the economy between positive and negative stories. Similarly, focusing on the columns, we get an impression of the differences between unemployment and inflation stories.

There are obvious differences between the means in the rows as well as in the columns. But without further computations, based on an underlying model, we cannot tell whether the differences are due to random variations or whether ratings of the economy are actually affected by the two explanatory variables. In order to develop the necessary formulas for a two-way analysis of variance, we need symbols for the observations and the various means. The symbols are shown in Table 8. Three subscripts are needed to show where an observation is located. The first subscript (i) refers to the row number, the second subscript (j) refers to the column number, and the third (k) counts the observations within a given cell. Since all the observations in the first row have 1 as the first subscript, the mean for those observations also has 1 as the first subscript; and similarly for the second row and the two columns.

Types of effects. Disregarding the columns in Table 7 for a moment, we find that the 6 subjects who saw the positive stories have a mean of 4.0, and those who saw the negative stories have a mean of 8.0. Since these means are different, the valence variable has an effect. A one-way analysis of variance can be used to see if this effect is statistically significant. The valence sum of squares becomes 48.0, and the residual sum of squares becomes 36.0. This results in a significant F of 13.33 on 1 and 10 degrees of freedom, and we conclude valence has an effect.

Similarly, disregarding the rows in Table 7, we see from the columns that the 6 subjects who saw the employment stories have a mean of 5.0,

TABLE 8
Rating Scores and Means of the Importance of the Economy,
by Issue and Valence, in Symbols

Valence of Coverage	Economic Issue Covered in Newscast		Mean
	Unemployment	Inflation	
Postive	y_{111} y_{112} y_{113} $(\bar{y}_{11})$	y_{121} y_{122} y_{123} $(\bar{y}_{12})$	$\bar{y}_{1.}$
Negative	y_{211} y_{212} y_{213} $(\bar{y}_{21})$	y_{221} y_{222} y_{223} $(\bar{y}_{22})$	$\bar{y}_{2.}$
Mean	$\bar{y}_{.1}$	$\bar{y}_{.2}$	$\bar{y}$

and the 6 subjects who saw the inflation stories have a mean of 7.0. Since the means are different, the issue variable may have a statistically significant effect. We can do a one-way analysis of variance to see if this effect is statistically significant. This analysis results in an issue sum of squares of 12.0 and a residual sum of squares of 72.0. These sum of squares give a nonsignificant F of 1.67 on 1 and 10 degrees of freedom, and we conclude the issue does not have an effect.

In addition to these two effects there is a possible third effect on the dependent variable called the interaction effect. It may be that issue and valence act together in such a way as to produce an effect over and beyond the separate effect of each of the two variables. Such an effect is present in the data in Table 7, and we see this effect in the four cell means.

For those who saw the positive stories, the difference in the means for the inflation story and the unemployment story is $6.0 - 2.0 = 4.0$. One way to look at this difference is to say that it measures the effect of issue. But if we look at the same difference for those who saw the negative stories, we find a difference of $8.0 - 8.0 = 0.0$. Thus the effect of the issue variable is 4.0 for the positive stories and 0.0 for the negative stories. The effect of the same variable is different for the two categories of the other variable. There is no unique effect of the issue variable, and the only reason the means are what they are must be that there is something else going on as well with these variables.

Similarly, if we look at the table the other way, we find that for the unemployment stories, the difference between the means for the negative and the positive stories is $8.0 - 2.0 = 6.0$, while the difference for the inflation stories is 8.0 – 6.0 = 2.0. Thus there is not the same effect in the two columns. This tells us that the four cell means cannot be fully explained by the effects of the issue plus valence. We continue the discussion of the interaction effect below.

Combined effect of both variables. The question now is whether we can do better than the two separate one-way analyses studying the effects of valence and issue. The answer is that we should not analyze the effects of the variables separately but together. This is achieved in a two-way analysis of variance.

The manipulations of a two-way analysis of variance can be broken into several stages. As a first step we can measure the total combined effect of the two explanatory variables. This is done by stringing out the data according to a combined variable, in our case a combined valence-issue variable, and measuring the effect of this combined variable using the methods from one-way analysis of variance. For our example the combined variable leads to four groups of observations, and the data and the results are shown in Table 9.

The analysis of variance table shows that the sum of squares for valence and issue together equals 72, and the residual sum of squares equals 12. Dividing the sums of squares by their degrees of freedom gives the two means squares, and their ratio gives F = 16.00 on 3 and 8 degrees of freedom. This value of F is significant at the 0.009 level; that is, the probability of getting an F-value this large or larger when the two variables have no effect equals as little as 0.009. One noticeable feature of this analysis is that the residual sum of square equals only 12.0, which is much smaller than the residual sums of squares we obtained for the two separate analyses.

In the general case with two explanatory variables A and B, where A has r categories and B has c categories, the number of categories for the combined A and B variable equals rc. Let n_{ij} denote the number of observations in the cell defined by the i-th category of A and the j-th category of B. The sum of squares for the combined A and B variable is then found according to the expression

$$\text{SS A and B} = \Sigma n_{ij}(\overline{y}_{ij} - \overline{y})^2$$

where the summation is across all cells. The total sum of squares is found, as before, by subtracting the overall mean from each observation, squaring these differences, and adding them all. Finally, the residual sum of squares is found as the difference between the total sum of squares and the sum of squares due to the combined A and B variable.

TABLE 9
Rating of Economy for Issue and Valence Analyzed
as a One-Way Analysis of Variance

	Unemployment Positive	Inflation Positive	Unemployment Negative	Inflation Negative
	1	5	7	7
	2	6	8	7
	3	7	9	10
Mean	2	6	8	8

Overall mean $\bar{y} = 6$

Source	Sum of Squares	Degrees of Freedom	Mean Square	F-ratio	Significance
Between groups	72	3	24.00	16.00	0.001
Within groups	12	8	1.50		
Total	84	11			

Three separate effects. The next step consists of decomposing the sum of squares for the combined variable into separate parts. One of these is the effect of the valence variable, and another is the effect of the issue variable.

To find the effect of the valence variable, we disregard the columns in Table 7 and do a one-way analysis of the rows. The two row means equal 4.0 and 8.0, and there are 6 observations in each row. With that, the sum of squares for the valence variable becomes

$$6(4.0 - 6.0)^2 + 6(8.0 - 6.0)^2 = 48.00$$

on 1 degree of freedom. This is the same sum of squares reported for the first separate analysis.

Similarly, to find the effect of the issue variable we disregard the rows in Table 7 and do a one-way analysis of variance for the columns. There are 6 observations in each column, and the two column means are 5.0 and 7.0. The overall mean equals 6.0. Thus the sum of squares for the issue variable becomes

$$6(5.0 - 6.0)^2 + 6(7.0 - 6.0)^2 = 12.00$$

on 1 degree of freedom. This is the same sum of squares as we found from the second separate analysis above.

The combined variable has a sum of squares equal to 72.00 on 3 degrees of freedom. Subtracting from that sum the separate sums of square for valence and issue leaves an amount equal to:

$$72.00 - 12.00 - 48.00 = 12.00$$

on $3 - 1 - 1 = 1$ degree of freedom. This is a sum of squares which measures the effect of valence and issue over and beyond their two separate effects, and this is known as the interaction effect. Valence and issue act together to produce an effect on people's view of the economy over and beyond their separate effects.

In the general case with r rows and c columns in the data table, the sum of squares for the combined A and B variable can also be decomposed into three components. The sum of squares for the A variable is found from the expression

$$SSA = \Sigma n_{i.} (\overline{y}_{i.} - \overline{y})^2 \qquad r - 1 \; df$$

where the summation is across all r categories of the A variable. Similarly, the sum of squares for the B variable is found from the expression

$$SSB = \Sigma n_{.j} (\overline{y}_{.j} - \overline{y})^2 \qquad c - 1 \; df$$

where the summation is across all c categories of the B variable. The sum of squares for the AB interaction variable can be found by subtracting the sums of squares for A and B from the sum of squares for the combined A and B variable. That is,

$$SSInteraction = SS \; A \; and \; B - SSA - SSB$$

on $(rc - 1) - (r - 1) - (c - 1) = (4 - 1)(c - 1)$ degrees of freedom. In our example $r = c = 2$, and the degrees of freedom for the sum of squares for the interaction equals 1.

Relationship between the explanatory variables. In order to examine the effects of the two categorical, explanatory variables on the metric, dependent variable, we need to turn to another aspect of two-way analysis of variance. This has to do with the relationship between the two explanatory variables themselves, here the relationship between economic issue (unemployment vs. inflation) and valence of coverage

TABLE 10
Contingency Table with Frequencies for Type and Valence

Valence of Coverage	Economic Issue Covered in Newscast		
	Unemployment	Inflation	Total
Positive	3	3	6
Negative	3	3	6
Total	6	6	12

(positive vs. negative). Since these are two categorical variables, their relationship can be examined by considering the contingency table formed by counting the number of observations in each cell of the table. This contingency table is seen in Table 10.

Since the four frequencies are all equal, the chi-square value for Table 10 equals zero, as does any of the correlation coefficients we might use to measure the strength of a relationship between two categorical variables. Thus, for the data in Table 10 there is no relationship between the two variables valence and issue. It should be emphasized that this value of chi-square has nothing to do with the possible effects of the two explanatory variables on the dependent variable. The chi-square analysis is concerned only with the possible relationship between the explanatory variables themselves.

The reason the two explanatory variables are unrelated here is that there is the same number of observations in each of the four cells in the data table. It can also be shown that when the cell frequencies are identical, the interaction variable is unrelated to the two explanatory variables. It is possible to have unequal cell frequencies and still have the two explanatory variables unrelated to each other, but in that case there is a relationship between the interaction variable and each of the explanatory variables.

Equality of cell frequencies is of great importance. When the two explanatory variables and the interaction variable are all unrelated, as they are in this example, it is possible to assess the unique effect of each of the three on the dependent variable in terms of their sums of squares. With unequal frequencies it is not possible to untangle the effects and get three unique sums of squares.

The same problem of unique effects also occurs in multiple regression analysis, where it is labeled the problem of collinearity. That name is not commonly used in connection with analysis of variance. Instead, there is usually a separate presentation of the analysis for the case of equal and unequal cell frequencies.

The problem of collinearity in analysis of variance is one reason why these methods have been little used in nonexperimental studies. In an experiment it is possible to assign equal number of subjects to the various categories of the explanatory variables. With observational data there is not the same freedom. Before collecting the data in a survey, for example, there is no way of knowing what the cell frequencies will be in a table, and most often they are not equal.

Analysis of variance table. The results of a two-way analysis of variance are commonly displayed in an analysis of variance table, and the results from our example is shown in Table 11. The table lists the sums of squares, degrees of freedom, mean squares, and F-ratios. As before, the means squares are found by dividing the sums of squares by their corresponding degrees of freedom. The F-ratios are obtained by dividing the first three means squares by the residual mean square. The table also includes E^2 for the different variables measuring the strengths of their relationship with the dependent variable, and those numbers are found by dividing each sum of squares by the total sum of squares.

The table shows that all three variables, valence, issue and interaction, have a significant effect on people's view of the economy. The highest significance is reached for the valence variable, and this variable also has the strongest relationship with the dependent variable.

The advantage of a two-way analysis of variance versus separate one-way analyses for the two explanatory variables is that with a two-way analysis, the effects of the two variables are pulled out of the residual variable at the same time. If, for example, we had used these data for a one-way analysis studying the effect of the issue variable, the issue sum of squares would have stayed the same at 12, with 1 degree of freedom. Also, the total sum of squares would have stayed the same at 84, with 11 degrees of freedom. But that leaves us with a residual sum of squares of 84 – 12 = 72, on 11 – 1 = 10 degrees of freedom. That way the residual means square becomes 72/10 = 7.20, and the F-ratio for the issue variable becomes 12/7.20 = 1.67 on 1 and 10 degrees of freedom. With our two-way analysis Table 11 shows an F for this variable of 8.00 on 1 and 8 degrees of freedom, and this F is considerably more significant.

TABLE 11
Analysis of Variance Table for the Data in Table 7

Source	Sum of Squares	Degrees of Freedom	Mean Square	F-ratio	Significance
Valence	48	1	48.0	32.00	0.0005
Issue	12	1	12.0	8.00	0.02
Interaction	12	1	12.0	8.00	0.02
Residual	12	8	1.5		
Total	84	11			

Valence $E^2 = 48/84 = 0.57$.
Issue $E^2 = 12/84 = 0.14$.
Interaction $E^2 = 12/84 = 0.14$.
Residual $E^2 = 12/84 = 0.14$.

Both the residual sum of squares and the residual degrees of freedom are smaller in a two-way than a one-way analysis of variance. The residual mean square is the ratio of the sum of squares and the degrees of freedom, and the smaller the mean square is, the larger is the resulting F-ratio. A smaller residual sum of squares in the two-way analysis leads to a smaller mean square; but at the same time, a smaller number of degrees of freedom leads to a larger mean square. From this discussion it is not entirely clear if there are any benefits doing a two-way analysis instead of a one-way analysis. However, if the second variable has any kind of effect on the dependent variable, the resulting reduction in the residual sum of squares more than offsets the reduction in its degrees of freedom, and the two-way analysis results in a smaller mean square and a larger F than the one-way analysis.

Effects of being in a particular row, column, and cell. The overall effects of the variables are shown in the sums of squares in Table 11. The valence variable is the most important, with a contribution of 48 to the total sum of squares. But this and the other sums of squares are overall measures, and they do not explain why it is that a particular observation has the value that it does. In addition to the sums of squares, we want to measure the effects of the variables on each of the observations.

The first observed value in the upper left cell of Table 7 equals 1. That observation equals 1 because that person has been affected by four effects:

(1) the story was on unemployment,
(2) the story was positive,

(3) the story was a positive unemployment story,

(4) the residual variable, that is, the net effect of all other variables.

Each of the twelve people were affected by the four variables in a similar way, and we see the presence of the effects in that the observations differ from each other. If the variables did not have any effects, the observations would all be equal.

We postulate that for a particular observation the four effects are additive, meaning that we can get any of the twelve observations in Table 7 by adding four effects, depending on which categories an observation belongs to. In order to better understand these variables, we would like to measure their effects for each of the categories. One way to get at the effects is to decompose the observed values, one step at a time, the way it is done below.

The first step consists of subtracting the overall mean $\overline{y}$ (= 6) from each observation. That centers the data, and it becomes a little easier to find the various effects. The resulting scores are shown in Table 12. The four types of effects are still just as present, since we only subtracted a constant in order to make the overall mean equal to zero.

Let us consider the effect of the valence variable, which defines the rows in the data table. The mean of the first row equals –2.0, and we interpret that to say that a value of 2.0 has been subtracted from the score of each person who saw a positive story. Thus the effect of seeing a positive story equals –2.0. Similarly, the mean of the second row equals 2.0, and we say that the effect of seeing a negative story equals 2.0.

In symbols, let $\hat{\alpha}_1$ denote the estimated effect of being in the first row of the table (positive story) and $\hat{\alpha}_2$ the effect of being in the second row (negative story). We find these effects from the expressions

$$\hat{\alpha}_1 = \overline{y}_1. - \overline{y} = 4 - 6 = -2$$
$$\hat{\alpha}_2 = \overline{y}_2. - \overline{y} = 8 - 6 = 2$$

where $\overline{y}_1.$ and $\overline{y}_2.$ are the original means of rows 1 and 2. In the general case the effect of the i-th category of the row variable is found as the difference between the row mean $\overline{y}_i.$ and the overall mean y. Because the effects are measured this way, the effects are restricted in such a way that when each effect is multiplied by the number of observations in the same row, then the sum of these products equals zero.

Now that the effects of positive and negative stories have been identified, we can subtract these effects and see what, if anything, remains to be explained. By subtracting –2 from all the observations in

TABLE 12
Rating Scores and Means of the Importance of the Economy
by Issue and Valence after Subtracting Overall Mean

Valence of Coverage	Economic Issue Covered in Newscast								Mean
	Unemployment				Inflation				
Positive	−5	−4	−3	(−4.0)	−1	0	1	(0.0)	−2.0
Negative	1	2	3	(2.0)	1	1	4	(2.0)	2.0
Mean		−1.0				1.0			0.0

the first row and 2 from all the observations in the second row of Table 12, we get the data in Table 13.

The two row means are now the same and equal to zero because the row effects have been subtracted from the data. But the four cell means are still different, as are the column means. Since the column mean for unemployment equals −1, the effect of seeing a story on unemployment has the effect of subtracting 1. Similarly, the effect of seeing a story on inflation has the effect of adding 1. Thus the effects of being in columns 1 and 2 can be measured by the column mean minus the overall mean, in this case

$$\hat{\beta}_1 = \overline{y}_{.1} - \overline{y} = 5 - 6 = -1$$
$$\hat{\beta}_2 = \overline{y}_{.2} - \overline{y} = 7 - 6 = 1$$

In the general case the effect of the j-th category of the column variable is found as the difference between the column mean $\overline{y}_{.j}$ and the overall mean $\overline{y}$. The restriction on these effects is such that when each effect is multiplied by the number of observations in the same column, then the sum of these products equals zero.

Next we subtract the effect of the unemployment story from all the observations in the first column in Table 13 and the effect of the inflation story from all the observations in the second column. This takes out the column effects and leaves us with the data in Table 14.

Now we have subtracted from each observation the effect of being in a particular row and the effect of a particular column. In Table 14 the row means and the column means are all zero, and this verifies that there are no row or column effects in the data any longer. A two-way analysis of variance on the data in Table 14 would give row and column sums of

TABLE 13
**Rating Scores and Means of the Importance of the Economy by
Issue and Valence after Subtracting Overall Mean and Row Effects**

Valence of Coverage	Economic Issue Covered in Newscast								Mean
	Unemployment				Inflation				
Positive	−3	−2	−1	(−2.0)	1	2	3	(2.0)	0.0
Negative	−1	0	1	(0.0)	−1	−1	2	(0.0)	0.0
Mean		−1.0				1.0			0.0

TABLE 14
**Rating Scores and Means of the Importance of the Economy by
Issue and Valence after Subtracting Overall Mean,
Row Effects, and Column Effects**

Valence of Coverage	Economic Issue Covered in Newscast								Mean
	Unemployment				Inflation				
Positive	−2	−1	0	(−1.0)	0	1	2	(1.0)	0.0
Negative	0	1	2	(1.0)	−2	−2	1	(−1.0)	0.0
Mean		0.0				0.0			0.0

squares equal to zero, indicating no effects. But the interaction and residual effects are still present, and a two-way analysis of variance of the data in Table 14 gives the same interaction and residual sums of squares as we have in the original analysis in Table 11.

The four cell means give us clues to the magnitudes of the effects of the interaction variable. The mean score for those who saw a positive story on unemployment is still equal to −1, even after we have subtracted the effect of the story being about unemployment as well as the effect of the story being positive. If those were the only two variables that had any effect, we would expect the mean in each cell to equal zero after the two effects have been taken out. But the mean in the first cell is still equal to −1, and it must be the interaction variable that brought the mean from 0 to −1. Thus the effect of the interaction variable for a positive unemployment story equals −1. Similarly, the effect of the interaction variable for positive inflation stories equals 1, for negative unemployment stories it also equals 1, and for negative inflation stories it equals −1.

The interaction effects can also be expressed in formulas. To find the effects we subtracted the overall mean $\overline{y}$ as an estimate of the overall constant μ, the row effect $\hat{\alpha}_i$, and the column effect $\hat{\beta}_j$. In symbols, the interaction effects $\hat{\gamma}_{ij}$ can be found from the equations

Positive unemployment:
$$
\begin{aligned}
\hat{\gamma}_{11} &= 2 - 6 - (-2) - (-1) \\
&= \overline{y}_{11} - \hat{\mu} - \hat{\alpha}_1 - \hat{\beta}_1 \\
&= \overline{y}_{11} - \overline{y} - (\overline{y}_{1.} - \overline{y}) - (\overline{y}_{.1} - \overline{y}) \\
&= \overline{y}_{11} - \overline{y}_{1.} - \overline{y}_{.1} + \overline{y} \\
&= 2 - 4 - 5 + 6 = -1
\end{aligned}
$$

Positive inflation:
$$
\begin{aligned}
\hat{\gamma}_{12} &= 6 - 6 - (-2) - 1 \\
&= \overline{y}_{12} - \hat{\mu} - \hat{\alpha}_1 - \hat{\beta}_2 \\
&= \overline{y}_{12} - \overline{y}_{1.} - \overline{y}_{.2} + \overline{y} = 1
\end{aligned}
$$

Negative unemployment:
$$
\begin{aligned}
\hat{\gamma}_{21} &= \overline{y}_{21} - \hat{\mu} - \hat{\alpha}_2 - \hat{\beta}_1 \\
&= \overline{y}_{21} - \overline{y}_{2.} - \overline{y}_{.1} + \overline{y} = -1
\end{aligned}
$$

Negative inflation:
$$
\begin{aligned}
\hat{\gamma}_{22} &= \overline{y}_{22} - \hat{\mu} - \hat{\alpha}_2 - \hat{\beta}_2 \\
&= \overline{y}_{22} - \overline{y}_{2.} - \overline{y}_{.2} + \overline{y} = 1
\end{aligned}
$$

In general, the estimate of the interaction effect for the cell located in the i-th row and j-th column of the table is found by taking the cell mean and subtracting the means of the corresponding row and column and, finally, adding the overall mean. This gives us the formula

$$
\hat{\gamma}_{ij} = \overline{y}_{ij} - \overline{y}_{i.} - \overline{y}_{.j} + \overline{y}
$$

for the interaction effect. Note that the sum of the interaction effects equals zero for any column and any row.

The residual variable. Finally we can subtract the interaction effects from the remaining parts of the observations. The results are given in Table 15. By now the only thing left of the original observations are the effects due to the residual variable. The effect of the residual variable on the first observation in the cell for the positive unemployment story equals –1, 0 for the second observation, etc.

From the way the various effects have been subtracted, it follows that the residuals in Table 15 are obtained as deviations of the original observations from the means of the observations in the corresponding cells. This is not surprising, because if the only variables operating here were the valence of newscast, issue of newscast, and valence-issue interaction, then all the observations in a particular cell would be equal. The extent to which the observations in a cell differ from each other must be due to the residual variable.

One of the formal assumptions of analysis of variance is again that the residuals form a normal distribution. The numbers we have here are only the estimated values of the residual variable, but their distribution is approximately normal if the true residuals are normal. Figure 6 shows the frequency distribution of our residuals. The distribution is skewed, but it does not offer any strong evidence against normality, particularly because we have such a small number of observations.

The assumption of normality is needed for the F-tests. Experience has shown that the F-tests are not adversely affected by minor deviations from normality in the distribution of the residuals. But even though the F-tests have been found to be robust in this sense, one should still examine the distribution of the residuals. One should watch for skewness and single values that lie far away from the rest of the data. For a further discussion of the analysis of residuals, see Anscombe and Tukey (1963). For a similar discussion of decompositions of effects, see Cobb (1984).

Sums of squares from effects. The smaller the residuals are, the better the analysis of variance model fits. We would therefore like to have an overall sense of how large the residuals are. But the mean of the residuals is always equal to zero and gives no indication of the magnitude of the residuals. Instead we turn to the squared residuals, and the sum of the squared residuals in Table 15 becomes

$$(-1)^2 + 0^2 + \ldots + 2^2 = 12$$

This is the same sum of squared residuals we have in the analysis reported in Table 11.

The variance of the residuals can be thought of as the average squared residual, and it is found by dividing the sum of squared residuals by the residual degrees of freedom. Here we have 8 degrees of freedom, and in general there are n– rc degrees of freedom, where n is the total number of

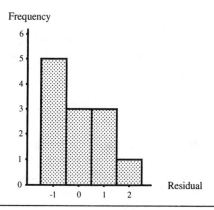

Figure 6: Histogram of Residuals in Table 15

TABLE 15
Rating Scores and Means of the Importance of the Economy by Issue and Valence after Subtracting Overall Mean, Row, Column, and Interaction Effects

Valence of Coverage	Economic Issue Covered in Newscast								Mean
	Unemployment				Inflation				
Positive	−1	0	1	(0.0)	−1	0	1	(0.0)	0.0
Negative	−1	0	1	(0.0)	−1	−1	2	(0.0)	0.0
Mean		0.0				0.0			0.0

observations, r the number of rows, and c the number of columns in the data table. In this case the variance becomes $s^2 = 12/8 = 1.5$, and the standard deviation $s = 1.2$. Thus a typical observation deviates 1.2 units from the mean in the cell in which it is located. Since the original observations range in values from 1 to 10, a deviation of 1.2 is quite small.

The other sums of squares in Table 11 can also be found from the effects we have identified. For valence we found that the effect of a positive story is −2 and a negative story is 2. Six people were given the −2 effect and the other six the 2 effect. Squaring the effects and adding them up for all twelve people gives the sum of squares

$$6(-2)^2 + 6(2)^2 = 48$$

for the valence variable. For the issue variable there are six people with a −1 effect and six others with a 1 effect. The overall effect of this variable then becomes

$$6(-1)^2 + 6(1)^2 = 12$$

Finally, the interaction sum of squares can be found from the four interaction effects −1, 1, −1, and 1 by squaring the effects, multiplying each square by the number of observations in the corresponding cell, and adding the products. That is,

$$3(-1)^2 + 3(1)^2 + 3(-1)^2 + 3(1)^2 = 12$$

which is the same interaction sum of squares we found in Table 11.

Formal model. This discussion started by focusing on the first observed value in the upper left cell of Table 7. Above we have found the effects that added together produce the observed value 1.0. This can be written, in words,

Observation = overall mean
+ effect of positive story
+ effect of unemployment story
+ effect of positive unemployment story
+ effect of residual variable

In numbers,

$$1 = 6 + (-2) + (-1) + (-1) + (-1)$$

and similarly for each of the eleven other observations. The magnitudes of these effects help us analyze the relative importance of the effects of the explanatory variables on the dependent variable, both directly for each of the categories of the explanatory variables and in an overall way for each variable by the corresponding sums of squares.

The decomposition above follows from the underlying theoretical model for a two-way analysis of variance. This model is an equation containing terms for the observed data and the different effects we have identified as the ones that together determine the data. The equation is written in such a way as to represent the actual real world process that produces the data. Two-way analysis of variance, as we discuss it here, makes use of an additive model, where the effects are added together to produce the data. That is, the k-th observed value located in the i-th row and j-th column of the data table can be written as the sum

$$y_{ijk} = \mu + \alpha_i + \beta_j + \gamma_{ij} + \epsilon_{ijk}$$

where μ is a constant

α_i is the effect of the i-th category of the row variable

β_j is the effect of the j-th category of the column variable

γ_{ij} is the effect of the (i, j)-th category of the interaction variable

ϵ_{ijk} is the effect of the residual variable

The mu, alphas, betas, and gammas are the parameters in this model. The formulas involving the various means we have for the effects are estimators of the model parameters. Numerical estimates of the parameters are obtained from our particular sample. The estimates are all found using the criterion that the sum of squared residuals should be as small as possible.

It is worth noting that the model we use is only one of many possible competing models. It could be, for example, that the effects act in a multiplicative way to generate the data or maybe in an exponential way. The advantage of the additive model is that it is much simpler to work with, but it should only be used if we think that the additive process is appropriate for the phenomenon we are studying.

Hypothesis testing. If the explanatory variables have any effect on the dependent variable, then the corresponding alphas, betas, and gammas are different from zero. While we do not have the true values of these parameters, we can use the observed data and the estimated parameter values to test hypotheses about the parameters and thereby reach conclusions about whether they are equal to zero or not.

One null hypothesis is that there are no row (valence) effects, i.e., that there is no difference between positive and negative stories and that the alphas are all equal to zero. This hypothesis can be expressed

$$H_0: \alpha_1 = \alpha_2 \ (= 0)$$

Because the estimated alphas are measured as deviations from the overall mean, some of the estimates will be negative and some will be positive. The weighted sum of the estimated effects, where the weights are the number of observations in each category, is equal to zero. Thus the only way the effects can be equal is for them all to be equal to zero. Another way of stating the same hypothesis is that the population means of the dependent variable are the same for all categories of the row variable.

This null hypothesis is tested by the F-value for valence in the analysis of variance table in Table 11, where $F = 32.00$. When we take the ratio of the row expected mean square and the residual expected mean square, we get the expression

$$1.00 + (6\alpha_1^2 + 6\alpha_2^2)/\sigma^2$$

where σ^2 is the variance of the residuals. The computed value of F is an estimate of the value of this expression. If the null hypothesis is true and the alphas really are equal to zero, then the value of this expression equals 1.00. In that case the observed sample value of F will be fairly close to 1.00.

On the other hand, if the null hypothesis is false, then the expression above has to be larger than 1.00. In that case the sample value of F will probably also be larger than 1.00 and approximately equal to whatever the true value is of the expression above. Thus a small value of F around 1.00 will lead us to conclude that the hypothesis of no effects is true, and a large value will make us conclude that the hypothesis is false. The specific cutoff value for F for which we reject the hypothesis is found in tables of the F-distribution. In our example, where there is 1 degree of freedom for valence and 8 for the residuals, we reject the null hypothesis if F is larger than 5.32 with a 5% significance level and 11.26 with a 1% significance level. Thus our observed F of 32.00 is significant at the 1% level.

In the general case, where there are r instead of 2 categories of the row variable, c categories of the column variable, and n observations altogether, the observed F has $r-1$ and $n-rc$ degrees of freedom. The critical values of F are still found from the F-tables in the column headed by $r-1$ and the row headed by $n-rc$.

The null hypothesis that there are no differences between the categories that form the columns in the data table (here that there is no difference between stories on unemployment and inflation) is tested the same way. With c columns the null hypothesis states

$$H_0: \beta_1 = \beta_2 = \ldots = \beta_c (= 0)$$

It is tested by the F for the column variable (here economic issue) where F = 8.00. When we take the ratio of the column expected mean square and the residual expected mean square we get the expression

$$1.00 + (n_1\beta_1^2 + n_2\beta_2^2 + \ldots + n_c\beta_c^2)/(c-1)\sigma^2$$

where the n's are the numbers of observations in the various columns. The computed value of F is an estimate of the numerical value of this expression. As before, if the observed F is a good deal larger than 1.00, then the hypothesis is rejected. The critical value of F is found from the F-table, using c-1 and n-rc degrees of freedom. Rejecting the hypothesis means we conclude that at least some of the betas are different from zero. In our example F is so large that the hypothesis is rejected at the 5% but not at the 1% level.

Finally, it is possible to test whether all the interaction effects are equal to zero. The null hypothesis states that they are all equal, meaning that they all equal zero. In our example,

$$H_0: \gamma_{11} = \gamma_{12} = \gamma_{21} = \gamma_{22} \; (=0)$$

The hypothesis is tested by the F-ratio for interaction because that F is also an estimate of a quantity similar to the other two and involving the true gammas. In the general case the degrees of freedom for the F for interaction becomes $(r-1)(c-1)$ and n-rc.

If the test for interaction reveals no significance, the formal model can take that into account and leave out the interaction effects. The model can then be expressed in the equation

$$y_{ijk} = \mu + \alpha_i + \beta_j + \epsilon_{ijk}$$

and this is a simpler, additive model than the one containing interaction effects. Any observation is here determined only by the effect of being in a particular row plus the effect of being in a particular column, plus the effect of the residual variable. In such a case the residual sum of squares is recomputed, as discussed in the section at the end of the chapter on pooling nonsignificant sums of squares.

The interpretation of the data is more troublesome if one or both main effects (row and column effects) are not significant while the interaction effect is significant. But we cannot remove a variable from the analysis without also removing any interaction variable which the variable helped create. This makes it hard to remove nonsignificant main effects.

We also have to keep in mind that even a very large and significant F-value only tells us that the corresponding effects differ from zero. It does not tell us anything about how much the effects differ from zero, and that is usually what is of interest. The larger the F, the stronger is the evidence that the effects are not equal to zero. The magnitudes of the differences can only be established by computing the effects for each category and interpreting them relative to the substantive topic we are studying.

Related Explanatory Variables

Related variables. One of the great advantages of experimental studies is that we can decide how many observations to make of the dependent variable for each combination of the various factors. This manipulation of the explanatory variables makes it possible to have those variables unrelated to each other. In the previous section the experimenter assigned the same number of subjects to each combination of categories of the explanatory variables. With such a design one can assess the unique effect of each explanatory variable and its interactions on the dependent variables.

This is not the case with observational studies. Here the investigator exercises no control over how many cases fall in the various categories or combinations of categories of the explanatory variables; any attempt to impose controls on the number of cases would immediately invalidate the research. With a random sample of the mass public we cannot stipulate, for example, that the proportion of blacks experiencing unemployment is the same as the proportion doing so among whites. More likely we are faced with a relationship between race and unemployment as shown in Table 16; the entries are realistic while contrived to keep the arithmetic simple.

The table shows 3 of 5 blacks (60%) to have suffered unemployment as opposed to 2 of 10 whites (20%). This means race and unemployment are correlated in the sample, and with phi equal to 0.40 the relationship is moderately strong.

Suppose we were interested in studying the effects of race and unemployment on how important the economy is rated as a problem. Table 17 lists the rating responses on a ten-point scale for the individuals

TABLE 16
Relationship Between Unemployment and Race
(hypothetical sample)

		Unemployment Last 12 Months		
		Yes	No	Total
Race	Black	3	2	5
	White	2	8	10
	Total	5	10	15

phi = 0.40

in Table 16. The correlation between unemployment and race will affect the analysis of variance of these data.

Formal model and plan for analysis. The equation for the formal model of a two-way analysis of variance with correlated explanatory variables is the same as for an analysis with uncorrelated variables. A particular observation is thought to be generated as a sum of an overall level, a row effect, a column effect, an interaction effect, and a residual effect. The effects are measured by sums of squares, as before, and the possible statistical significance of the effects are determined by F-ratios.

The major difference lies in the fact that a given variable does not necessarily have a unique sum of squares measuring the effect of that variable. The total sum of squares TSS is found as before, the sum of squared deviations of the observations from the overall mean. Similarly, the residual sum of squares RSS is found as the sum of squared deviations of the observations from their cell means. The difference TSS–RSS represents the combined effect of the row variable, column variable, and interaction variable. We would like to break this quantity into three parts, one for each of the three variables, but it is not possible to do that in a unique way.

The general approach is to deal with one of the variables at a time, find the sum of squares for that variable, and then allocate the remaining sum to the other variables. That way the sums of squares will depend on the order in which we let a variable enter the analysis. This is the same way collinearity is dealt with in stepwise regression.

Sums of squares. To show how the sums of squares for a two-way analysis of variance with unequal cell frequencies are computed, we use the data in Table 17 as an example. In order to simplify the discussion, this example is constructed such that there is no interaction effect

TABLE 17
Rating Scores and Means of the Importance of the Economy,
by Race and Unemployment

		Yes				No					Mean
Race	Black	7	8	9	(8.0)	2	6			(4.0)	6.4
	White	5	7		(6.0)	1	1	1	2	(2.0)	2.8
						2	3	3	3		
	Mean		7.2				2.4				4.0

Column header (spanning Yes/No): **Unemployed Last 12 Months**

present. We can see this from the four cell means because the difference between the means for blacks and whites equals 2.0 both in the yes and the no column.

The means in Table 17 suggest that blacks express more concern over the economy than do whites. The sum of squares due to race, reflecting this difference, can be found from the means in Table 17 and becomes

$$\text{RaceSS} = n_1.(\bar{y}_1. - \bar{y})^2 + n_2.(\bar{y}_2. - \bar{y})^2$$
$$= 5(6.4 - 4.0)^2 + 10(2.8 - 4.0)^2 = 43.20$$

There is also a difference in the means between those unemployed and not. The effect of the unemployment variables can be measured by the sum of squares

$$\text{UnemplSS} = n_{.1}(\bar{y}_{.1} - \bar{y})^2 + n_{.2}(\bar{y}_{.2} - \bar{y})^2$$
$$= 5(7.2 - 4.0)^2 + 10(2.4 - 4.0)^2 = 76.80$$

Adding these two effects gives a total of 120.00. At the same time, the computation of the total sum of squares results in TSS = 106.00. Since the sum of the effects cannot exceed the total sum of squares, we must modify the estimation of the effects of race and unemployment in some way.

It is possible to find the combined effect of race and unemployment just as we did for two unrelated variables in Table 9. We can string out the two variables in a combined variable with four categories and do a one-way analysis on the data when they are arranged that way. This gives the following sum of squares for the combined variable:

$$Race\&UnemplSS = 3(8.0 - 4.0)^2 + 2(4.0 - 4.0)^2$$
$$+ 2(6.0 - 4.0)^2 + 8(2.0 - 4.0)^2$$
$$= 88.00$$

Thus the whole is smaller than the sum of the parts. The sum of squares for both variables taken together equals 88.0, while the sum of the two separate sums of squares equals 120.0. The reason for this is that race and unemployment are correlated with each other, and this correlation stands in the way of our attempt to measure the separate effects of the two variables.

There are two options available for solving this problem. One, we can measure the effect of race first and then measure the effect of unemployment after race has been permitted to explain what it can. On the other hand, we can do the reverse and measure the effect of unemployment first and then allocate the remaining part of the combined effect to race. SPSS allows for both these arrangements.

The results are shown in Table 18. In both cases the sums of squares for race and unemployment add up to 88.00, but we use the separate sums of squares above as the first entry in the analysis of variance table. As is to be expected, the total and residual sums of squares are not affected by the way in which we divide the sums of squares for race and unemployment.

The importance of order. The example shows the importance of the order in which the variables are introduced. When an analysis like this is done on a computer, it is important that the output specifies in which order the variables have been entered in the analysis.

Which of these two results one chooses depends on reasoning that cannot be supplied by the analysis of variance. Instead, it must come from the substantive theory concerning the causal connections among the variables. For this example one might want to consider which of the two explanatory variables is exogenous. Clearly, race is not something that could be caused by unemployment, while it is possible to argue that race affects one's employment opportunities. Hence one could consider the effect of race first and then measure the effect of unemployment with the race effect removed. These are the results in the upper table in Table 18.

TABLE 18
Analysis of Variance Tables for Example
with Correlated Explanatory Variables

		Option 1			
Source	Sum of Squares	Degrees of Freedom	Mean Square	F-ratio	Significance
Race	43.20	1	43.20	28.80	0.0002
Unemployment, after Race	44.80	1	44.80	29.90	0.0001
Residual	18.00	12	1.50		
Total	106.00	14			
		Option 2			
Unemployment	76.80	1	76.80	51.20	0.00001
Race, after Unemployment	11.20	1	11.20	7.50	0.018
Residual	18.00	12	1.50		
Total	106.00	14			

Another approach consists of taking whatever variable has the largest sum of squares as the first variable and allocating the remaining effect to the next variable. This corresponds to the usual stepwise regression, which chooses the explanatory variables in the order of their sums of squares. In our example that argues for unemployment as the first variable with an effect of 76.80. After unemployment, race has only a small additional effect of 11.20. These are the results shown in the lower table in Table 18.

Not only do the sums of squares change when the order of the variables is changed. From the changing sums of squares we get changing mean squares and thereby changing F-ratios. In our example all the F-ratios are significant, but it is very possible to imagine cases where a variable is found to be significant if it is included first in the analysis and not significant if it enters the analysis later.

One way to interpret the differing sums of squares is to say that there is a part of the combined sum of squares of 88.00 that is shared by the two explanatory variables. The sum of squares for race drops from 43.20

to 11.20 when the variable is entered first versus when it is entered as the second variable. This is a drop of 32.00. Similarly, the sum of squares for unemployment drops from 76.80 to 44.80, and this is also a drop of 32.00.

This shared part and the other sums of squares are illustrated in Figure 7. The area in the middle represents the portion of the variation in the dependent variable shared by both variables. The two outside areas illustrate those parts of the variation that each variable explains alone, after the other variable has entered the analysis first. Each of the explanatory variables loses a sizable share of its sum of squares when it is entered after the other variable. This is so because the two explanatory variables are related to each other as well as to the dependent variable.

Interaction. In order to keep the example simple, there was no

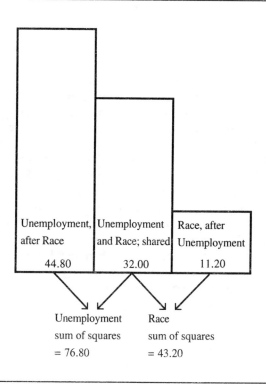

Figure 7: Partitioning of Variation due to Unemployment and Race

interaction effect built into the data. The presence or absence of interaction has nothing to do with the correlation or lack thereof between the explanatory variables. Interaction is an effect on the dependent variable over and beyond the separate effects of the explanatory variables, and it can exist whether or not the explanatory variables themselves are correlated.

The presence of an interaction effect is seen in the patterns of the cell means; and when there is interaction, we must also include an interaction sum of squares. In that case the computations get considerably more cumbersome, and we do not include the necessary formulas here. The interaction sum of squares is always computed in such a way that the explanatory variables themselves are allowed to explain as much of the variation in the dependent variable as possible before the interaction variable is entered.

Special Topics

One observation per cell. There are times when each combination of the explanatory variables has only one observation of the dependent variable. That is, there is only one observation in each cell in the data table. This situation cannot be handled by the methods discussed so far. The two nominal variables would be uncorrelated in this case, since the number of observations is the same in each cell. But another problem arises instead, and it would not be possible to compute any F-ratios and thereby test any hypotheses about the presence of effects.

It would not be possible to do any testing because we do not have any way of getting the denominator for the F-values. As we have seen, the denominator for the F's is the mean square for the residuals, obtained from the residual sum of squares. But each residual in that sum of squares is obtained from the difference between the observed score and the mean in the corresponding cell in the data table. With only one observation in the cell, the mean is equal to that observation, and the residual would be zero. With the residuals all equal to zero, the residual sum of squares and mean square become zero, and we cannot divide by zero.

The case with only one observation in each cell does not occur that often, but it is useful to consider this case for another reason. If we want to get some preliminary ideas of whether row and column effects are present or not without performing all the computations necessary for a complete analysis, we can first compute the mean of the dependent variable for the observations in each cell. By replacing the original observations with the cell means, we then have the case in which there is only one value in each cell. These means can then be analyzed for the presence of row and column effects as outlined below.

The way to do an analysis of variance with one observation in each cell is to make the assumption that there are no interaction effects present. This limits the analysis; but if this assumption is true, we can get a good sense of the row and column effects. Even when the assumption of no interaction is true, we can still compute an interaction sum of squares using the same formulas as before. This sum of squares can then be thought of as containing random effects, and it can be used as the residual sum of squares. By dividing this sum of squares by the proper degrees of freedom we get a mean square for the denominators of the F's for the row and column effects.

When we have unequal cell frequencies and correlated explanatory variables, this approach suggests reducing the data to the case with one observation in each cell and basing the analysis on the reduced data. That way we do not have to worry about the explanatory variables being related, and there is no problem with the order in which the variables are brought into the analysis.

The analysis is based on the assumption of nonsignificant interaction effects. Had we started with only one observation in each cell, it would not have been possible to determine whether the interaction effects are present or not. The worst that can happen is that there are significant interaction effects present, unknown to us. What we here have taken as the residual mean square would then have been the effect of the residual variable plus the effect of the interaction variable. That makes the denominator in the F-values too large, since it should only represent the effect of the residual variable. If the denominators are too large, then the F's are too small. The result of this is that we may not be able to detect that the row and column effects are significant, even if they really are significant. But if we still find significant F-values using a denominator that is too large, then we know that the significance level is on the conservative side.

As a small numerical example we return to Table 7 and take the cell means in that table as the single observations in the various cells. Thus we have the data shown in the top part of Table 19. A two-way analysis of variance of these four observations gives us the results shown in the lower part of Table 19. The results from the original analysis of variance are shown in Table 11.

TABLE 19
Two-Way Analysis of Variance with One Observation in Each Cell

Valence of Coverage	Economic Issue Covered in Newscast		
	Unemployment	Inflation	Mean
Positive	2.0	6.0	4.0
Negative	8.0	8.0	8.0
Mean	5.0	7.0	6.0

Source	Sum of Squares	Degrees of Freedom	Mean Square	F-ratio	Significance
Valence	16.0	1	16.0	4.00	0.295
Issue	4.0	1	4.0	1.00	0.50
Residual	4.0	1	4.0		
Total	24.00	3			

Several comments can be made about the analyses in Tables 11 and 19. In both cases valence emerges as the more important variable. Using all the observations, valence has an eta square of $48/84 = 57\%$; using only the cell means, it has an eta squared of $16/24 = 75\%$. While the two percentages are different, they are still in the same ball park. The F-ratios for valence and issue are both smaller in Table 19 than they are in Table 11, but they are not excessively different.

The major difference between the two analyses lies in the degrees of freedom for the residual. When we use all the observations, the degrees of freedom for the residual is mainly determined by the number of observations in the data. When we use the means as single observations, the degrees of freedom are determined by the size of the table. Because each variable has only two categories, we end up with as little as 1 degree of freedom for the residual in this example. The major drawback of a very small number of degrees of freedom for the residuals is that in order to be called significant, the F-ratio has to be very large. With a 5% significance the critical value for F on 1 and 1 degrees of freedom equals as much as 161.4. Thus the largest difference between the results in Tables 11 and 19 are found in the last column, where we see that the results in Table 11 are much more significant than the results in Table 19.

Thus it is possible to do analysis of variance with only one observation in each cell, whether that is a single observation or a mean; but the analysis works better if the explanatory variables have more than just two categories. With more categories we get more degrees of freedom for the residual sum of squares and smaller critical values of F.

Pooling nonsignificant sums of squares. There are times when the F-value for the interaction variable is not significant. We are then faced with the question of what produced the interaction sum of squares. One answer is that in this case, the interaction sum of squares is due to randomness in the data coming from the effect of other variables not included in the analysis. But that effect is already identified as the effect of the residual variable, and we also have the residual sum of squares as a measure of that effect. This means we now have two measures of the effect of the residual variable. When that is the case, it is better to combine the two effects of the residual variable into one.

The interaction and residual sums of squares are added together, and the sum is used as the new residual sum of squares. This is known as pooling of the sums of squares. We get the degrees of freedom for the new residual sum of squares by adding $(r-1)(c-1)$ from the interaction effect to $n-rc$ from the old residual effect. This equals $n-r-c+1$. By dividing the new residual sum of squares by its degrees of freedom, we get the new residual mean square; and it is usually smaller than the old residual mean square, resulting in larger values of F for the row and column effects.

In addition, a larger number of degrees of freedom for the F's means that the critical values from the F-table for the rejection of the null hypotheses get smaller. Thus, by pooling the sums of squares, we get larger F-values, and at the same time we need smaller values of F in order to find our results significant. These two advantages can make it very worthwhile pooling insignificant sums of squares.

Interaction as nonparallel lines. The interaction variable has been introduced as the joint effect of the two explanatory variables over and beyond the separate effects of the two variables. One way to display the presence of interaction is to draw a picture like Figure 8. The information in that graph is taken from the data in Table 7.

The picture is made the following way. The categories for one of the explanatory variables are marked off along the horizontal axis. It makes no difference which of the two is chosen. The dependent variable is marked off along the vertical axis. Next, each of the cell means is plotted in its appropriate place. Finally, connecting lines are drawn between the means that have the same category of the second explanatory variable.

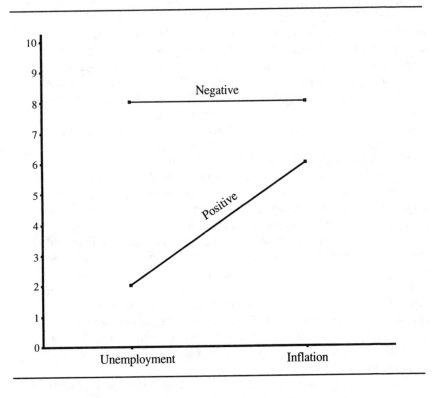

Figure 8: Means in Four Groups Pairwise connected by Lines, Showing Presence of Interaction

In our graph unemployment and inflation are chosen as two points on the horizontal axis, the negative means are connected by one line and the positive means are connected by another line.

The important feature of the two lines is that they are not parallel. That tells us there is an interaction effect present in the data. The fact that the lines are not parallel means that it makes a difference for the dependent variable whether we are dealing with unemployment or inflation stories. The figure shows that for unemployment there is a change of 6 units when we go from positive to negative stories. But for inflation there is only a change of 2 units from positive to negative stories. In other words, it makes a difference whether we are dealing with unemployment or inflation when we compare positive and negative stories. This is only another way of stating that we have interaction effects in these data.

4. ANALYSIS OF VARIANCE, SAMPLE OF CATEGORIES

One-Way Analysis

Sample of categories. The type of analysis of variance outlined in Chapters 2 and 3 is called model I type analysis. That model is also known as a fixed model. We now turn to model II, also called the random effect model. The main difference between the two models is that model II does not require observations on the dependent variable for every one of the categories of the explanatory variable(s). Instead, model II handles situations where data are collected only for a sample of categories.

Such a situation occurs in research trying to determine whether or not the order of presentation makes a difference to the way people respond to questions in an interview. Let us continue with the problem of how important an issue individuals rate the economy. This is a broad area, and the entire interview consists of more than just one question on the economy. There might be questions on approval rating of the president, partisanship, political interest, economic well-being, and of course the importance of other issues.

It might well matter for the rating of the economy where among the other items this question is placed in the interview. Suppose we are concerned with the ordering of six particular questions in the interview schedule. These questions can be ordered in a staggering 720 different ways. This number is so large that there is no way we could use all of them in an experiment on the ordering of questions. The only possibility is to draw a sample of orderings and restrict our experiment to those particular orderings. Thus we are prepared to take a random sample from the 720 permutations and assign subjects randomly to each of those permutations of questions. Say we sample 5 such question orders and assign 4 subjects to each order.

Table 20 presents the rating responses furnished by those 20 subjects. Since these 5 orderings, numbered 1 through 5, form a randomly chosen sample of orderings selected from the larger population of all 720 orderings, we are no longer as interested as before in the specific effect of each ordering on the rating of the economy. We can still find the effect of each ordering by taking the difference between the ordering mean and the overall mean, but these effects now form a random sample from a larger set of effects. In other words, these five values have been sampled from a random variable that would have provided different values if other orderings had been selected instead. Because of this, a model II analysis is also called a random effect model as opposed to a fixed effect model.

We are interested in the question of whether the ordering a subject was exposed to has an effect on the rating score. This implies a null hypothesis which states that all the ordering effects are equal to zero. Analysis of variance model II offers a test of this hypothesis by determining whether the variance of all the effects equals zero. The only way a variance can equal zero is for all the values (taken as deviations from the mean) to equal zero themselves.

Formal model and computations. The formal structures of models I and II look very similar for a one-way analysis, and the computations are identical. But, in addition, a random model permits the estimation of the new concept of the variance of the effect for all the elements in the population.

The formal model for a model II analysis states that the j-th observation in the i-th group, y_{ij}, is equal to the overall mean μ, plus the effect of being in the i-th group, plus the effect of all other variables. This is expressed in the equation

$$y_{ij} = \mu + a_i + \epsilon_{ij}$$

where a_i is the effect of the explanatory variable in the i-th group (here ordering), and ϵ_{ij} is the effect of the residual variable on this particular observation.

The model also specifies that the distribution of the a's in the population of all the a's forms a normal distribution with mean zero and variance σ_a^2. In principle this requires an infinitely large population of a's, even though our example is restricted to a population of 720 a-values. Similarly, the residual variable is assumed to have a normal distribution with mean zero and variance σ^2. A random model like the one we are dealing with here also requires the same number of

TABLE 20
Hypothetical Data for an Example of One-Way Analysis of
Variance, Model II, and the Resulting Analysis of Varaince Table

	Question Ordering				
	1	2	3	4	5
	8	5	7	9	6
	7	4	6	8	5
	6	3	5	7	4
	5	2	4	6	3
Mean	6.5	3.5	5.5	7.5	4.5

Overall mean = 5.5

Source	Sum of Squares	Degrees of Freedom	Mean Square	F-ratio	Significance
Between orderings	40.00	4	10.00	6.00	0.004
Within orderings	25.00	15	1.67		
Total	65.00	19			

$s^2 = 1.67$; $s_a^2 = 2.08$.

observations in each group; a requirement not encountered in a model I
type of analysis. In our example each group has n = 4 observations.

The hypothesis we want to test is that ordering has no effect on the
dependent variable. When ordering has no effect, then all the a's are
equal to zero. In that case the variance of the a's is also equal to zero. The
null hypothesis of σ_a^2 equal to zero can be tested by the same F-ratio used
for the model I type of analysis in Chapter 2.

First we find the total sum of squares by computing the difference
between each observation and the overall mean, squaring all the
differences, and adding up the squares. That is,

$$TSS = \Sigma (y_{ij} - \overline{y})^2$$
$$= (8 - 5.5)^2 + (7 - 5.5)^2 + \ldots + (3 - 5.5)^2 = 65.00$$

Similarly, the between-group sum of squares for ordering is found by
taking the difference between each group mean and the overall mean,

squaring all the differences, multiplying each square by the number of observations in each group, and adding all the products. That is,

$$BSS = \Sigma n(\bar{y}_i - \bar{y})^2$$
$$= 4(6.5 - 5.5)^2 + \ldots + 4(4.5 - 5.5)^2 = 40.00$$

Finally, the within group sum of squares for the residual variable can be found as the difference of the total sum of squares and the between-group sum of squares, here WSS = 65.00 − 40.00 = 25.00.

The degrees of freedom are the same as for a model I analysis. The degrees of freedom for the total sum of squares equals the number of observations minus one, for the between-group sum of squares the number of groups minus one, and for the within-group sum of squares the number of observations minus the number of groups. For our examples these numbers are 19, 4, and 15, respectively.

The mean squares are found by dividing the sums of squares by their degrees of freedom. It can then be shown that for a random model the between-group mean square, here equal to 10.00, is an estimate of the quantity $\sigma^2 + n\sigma_a^2$, where σ^2 is the population variance of the residuals and σ_a^2 the population variance of the a's. This quantity is also known as the group expected mean square. It can also be shown that the residual mean square is an estimate of σ^2, also known as the residual expected mean square. These two estimates now make it possible to draw conclusions about σ_a^2.

Dividing the between-group mean squares by the residual mean square gives us an F-ratio estimating the quantity $1.00 = n\sigma_a^2/\sigma^2$. If the variance of the a's really is equal to zero, the observed ratio calculated from our sample data should lie in the neighborhood of 1.00. On the other hand, if σ_a^2 really is not equal to zero, then the observed ratio ought to be larger than 1.00. This means that the observed value of the F-ratio can give us a clue about whether the null hypothesis is true or not. For values of F around 1.00 the null hypothesis is not rejected, and for values somewhat larger than 1.00 it is rejected. In our example the observed value of F becomes F = 10.00 / 1.67 = 6.00, which is considerably larger than 1.00. In order to decide whether a particular value of F is large enough for the null hypothesis of a zero variance of the a's to be rejected, we consult tables for the F distribution. The F-table tells us that when the hypothesis of a zero variance is true, the probability is only 0.05 of observing an F-value of 3.06 or larger. Since we observed F equal to 6.00, we reject the null hypothesis. Thus ordering does affect the rating scores of the economy, and this goes for the population of all orderings, not just the five orderings in the sample.

Estimating variance components. The rejection of the null hypothesis establishes that the explanatory variable has an effect on the dependent variable. The next question is how to measure how large this effect is.

One such measure is provided by the proportion of the between sum of squares to the total sum of squares, which in our example is $40.00/65.00 = 0.62$. The ordering variable, therefore, explains 62% of the total variation in the ratings of the economy. Another, and related, way of measuring the effect of the ordering variable would be to estimate the effects (the a's) for each of the five orderings in the sample. These a's can be estimated by the differences between the ordering means and the overall mean; that is, $\hat{a}_1 = 6.5 - 5.5 = 1.0$, $\hat{a}_2 = 3.5 - 5.5 = -2.0$, and so on.

One difficulty with these numbers is that they do not tell us anything about the magnitudes of the a's for all the other orderings in the population. Also, their magnitudes cannot be summarized by their mean, since their sum is always equal to zero. Instead of measuring how large the effect is of the ordering variable this way, we turn to the variance of the a's instead. Since the mean of the a's is zero, we know that the larger the variance is, the larger are the a's.

In order to estimate the variance of the a's we make use of the group and residual mean squares. Since the group mean square equals 10.00 and the residual mean square equals 1.67, we have the following expressions,

$$10.00 \cong \sigma^2 + 4\sigma_a^2 \qquad \text{and} \qquad 1.67 \cong \sigma^2$$

where the quantities on the left are only estimates of and not exactly equal to the expected mean squares on the right. Now we can solve the two expressions for the two variances and get the following estimated variance components

$$s^2 = 1.67 \qquad \text{and} \qquad s_a^2 = (10.00 - 1.67)/4 = 2.08$$

Since the variance of the a's exceeds the variance of the residuals, on the average the a-values are larger than the residuals. Another way to measure the effects is to take the square roots of the estimated variances and consider the standard deviations. The standard deviation of the a's becomes 1.44, and this is a number that can be taken as the average ordering effect. Thus a typical ordering differs by almost one and a half rating points from the overall mean for all orderings.

There is little difference between a fixed and a random one-way analysis of variance. The computations and the F-ratios are the same, and the only differences are that the random model requires the same number of observations in each group and that it permits the computations of variance components. The two models differ more when there are two explanatory variables rather than just one.

Two Explanatory Variables

Formal model and computations. A random effects model of analysis of variance with two explanatory variables is based on the same ideas as the random model with only one explanatory variable. The categories of both explanatory variables are samples from much larger populations of categories, and the aim of the analysis is to assess the effects of the explanatory variables on the dependent variable.

Let us continue the example from the previous section and add one more explanatory variable. In addition to the order of the questions, we suspect the probing of the importance of other issues may affect the rating subjects provide for the importance of the economy. Again, the number of possible items is large enough to defeat any reasonable effort to probe them all. To keep the example simple we draw a sample of two issues, denoted A and B, from an exhaustive list of issues on the political agenda. We cross this sample of two issues with the sample of five orderings and end up with ten experimental conditions. In other words, each of the five selected question orders is prefaced with the question regarding the importance of one of the two issues A or B. Table 21 displays the rating scores provided by the subjects, who were randomly assigned to each of the ten conditions.

The formal model for the analysis of data of this kind specifies that the k-th observation in the cell defined by the i-th row and the j-th column, y_{ijk}, can be written as the sum

$$y_{ijk} = \mu + a_i + b_j + c_{ij} + \epsilon_{ijk}$$

The various terms in this sum have very much the same interpretations as the corresponding terms in the fixed model for a two-way analysis of variance in Chapter 2. The parameter μ is a constant that centers the effects around zero. The next term, a_i, measures the effect of the i-th category of the row variable (issue), and the two issue effects are denoted

a_1 and a_2. These two quantities have been sampled from a large population of a-values, and it is assumed that the distribution of the a-values in the population is normal with mean zero and variances σ_a^2. In order to assess the effect of issue, we are not as concerned with the two values a_1 and a_2 as we are with the entire population of a-values. One way to specify in a null hypothesis that the variable has no effect is to specify that the population variance of the a's equals zero, because this implies that all the a-values in the population are equal to zero.

Similarly, the term b_j refers to the effect of the j-th category of the column variable (ordering). The five columns give rise to the five effects denoted b_1, b_2, b_3, b_4, and b_5. We assume, again, that the population of b's from which these five were sampled has a normal distribution with mean zero and variance σ_b^2. The null hypothesis that ordering has no effect gets translated into the statement that the variance of the b's equals zero.

The interaction effect, produced by the combination of the i-th row and the j-th column is captured by the term c_{ij}. With 10 cells in the data table there are 10 interaction terms. They are assumed to have been sampled from a population of interaction terms following a normal distribution with mean zero and variance σ_c^2. The null hypothesis of no interaction effect translates into the statement that the variance of the c's equals zero.

The residual term in the model, ϵ_{ijk}, measures the effect on rating scores stemming from all other variables. We assume that the 20 residuals in our example come from a population of residual terms with a normal distribution with mean zero and variance σ^2.

The five sums of squares, degrees of freedom, and mean squares are computed in the same way for a random model as they are for a fixed model. The results for our example are shown in the analysis of variance table in Table 21. The total sum of squares is the same for this analysis as it is for the one-way analysis above, and the ordering sum of squares is also unchanged in comparison with the results in Table 20 for the one-way analysis. But the old residual sum of squares of 25.00 on 15 degrees of freedom has visibly declined since the issue and interaction variables have been extracted. It now stands only at 11.00 on 10 degrees of freedom.

The major difference between a model I and a model II two-way analysis of variance lies in the computations of the F-ratios. Recall that for the model I type of analysis in Chapter 3, the F-ratios for the row variable, the column variable, and the interaction variable were each obtained by dividing the corresponding mean square by the mean

TABLE 21
**Hypothetical Data for an Example of Two-Way Analysis of
Variance, Model II, and the Resulting Analysis of Variance Table**

			Question Ordering			
	1	2	3	4	5	Mean
Issue						
A	8	5	7	9	6	
	7	4	6	8	5	5.9
B	6	3	5	7	4	
	5	2	4	6	3	5.1
Mean	5.5	4.5	3.5	6.5	7.5	5.5

Source	Sum of Squares	Degrees of Freedom	Mean Square	F-ratio	Significance
Issue	3.2	1	3.20	1.18	0.30
Ordering	40.0	4	10.00	3.70	0.04
Interaction	10.8	4	2.70	2.45	0.11
Residual	11.0	10	1.10		
Total	65.0	19			

F(issue) = 3.20/2.70 = 1.18.
F(ordering) = 10.00/2.70 = 3.70.
F(int) = 2.70/1.10 = 2.45.

square for the residual variable. This is no longer the case with a model II analysis.

Here the mean square for the row variable (issue) must be divided by the mean square for interaction in order to give an F-ratio for the row variable. Similarly, the F-ratio for the column variable (ordering) is obtained by dividing the column mean square by the interaction mean square. Finally, the interaction F is found by dividing the interaction mean square by the residual mean square. The reason the F-ratios are different in the random model has to do with the various mean squares estimates, as seen in the next section.

In the example the F-ratio for the row variable (issue) becomes 3.20/2.70 = 1.18, and for the column variable (ordering) it becomes 10.00/2.70 = 3.70. The interaction F becomes 2.70/1.10 = 2.45. Only the F for the column variable is significant at a 5% significance level.

It could make quite a difference whether a set of data is analyzed according to a random or a fixed model. If the row and column mean squares had been divided by the residual mean square instead, as required for a fixed model, we would have gotten F's of 2.91 and 9.09. Compared to the F's we got for the random model, we see that the fixed model would have shown the effects to be much more significant. But it is not that we have a choice between fixed and random model. It should always be clear from the way the data were collected which way the data should be analyzed.

Estimating variance components. In addition to seeing whether any of the variances of the effects equal zero, we often want to estimate the numerical values of the variances. These variances tell us how large the effects are, and they give a better sense of how well the substantive model explains the data than the results of the hypothesis tests.

In order to estimate the unknown variances, we need to know something about how they relate to quantities we can compute from the data. From the model for the two-way random model, it is possible to derive that the various mean squares and population variances are related in the following way:

The row mean square
is an estimate of
$$\sigma^2 + n\sigma_c^2 + nc\sigma_a^2$$

The column mean square
is an estimate of
$$\sigma^2 + n\sigma_c^2 + nr\sigma_b^2$$

The interaction mean square
is an estimate of
$$\sigma^2 + n\sigma_c^2$$

The residual mean square
is an estimate of
$$\sigma^2$$

where n is the number of observations in each cell, r the number of rows, and c the number of columns in the data table. The expressions on the right are the expected mean squares.

These expressions show why we compute the F-ratios the way we do. For example, by dividing the row mean square by the interaction mean square, we see from the estimates that we get something which estimates the quantity $1.00 +$ a ratio with σ_a^2 in the numerator. If the null hypothesis of no row effect is true, then that ratio is equal to 1.00, and F is just an estimate of 1.00. If this null hypothesis is not true and σ_a^2 is different from zero, then F is an estimate of something larger than 1.00. We see that the interaction mean square is used in the denominators for the row and column F's because both row and column mean squares estimate quantities that contain the interaction variance σ_c^2.

These expressions can be used to estimate the unknown effect variances. We replace the population variances by their sample estimates, using the letter s for estimates, and then we set the resulting expressions equal to the observed mean squares. That gives the four equations

$$3.2 = s^2 + 2s_c^2 + 10s_a^2$$
$$10.0 = s^2 + 2s_c^2 + 4s_b^2$$
$$2.7 = s^2 + 2s_c^2$$
$$1.1 = s^2$$

These equations can now be used to solve for the four estimated variances. The last equation shows that the variance of the residuals equals 1.10, and the standard deviation of the residuals becomes s = 1.05. From the next to the last equation we get, for the interaction effects,

$$s_c^2 = (2.7 - 1.1)/2 = 0.8 \qquad s_c = 0.89$$

Now we can use the first two equations to find the row and column estimated variances,

$$s_a^2 = (3.2 - 2.7)/10 = 0.05 \qquad s_a = 0.22$$
$$s_b^2 = (10.0 - 2.7)/4 = 1.82 \qquad s_b = 1.35$$

These estimates confirm our impressions from the F-values. The column variable emerges with the largest effect; an average column mean deviates from the overall mean by a value of 1.35 points. An average row mean deviates only by 0.22 points from the overall mean. Also, there is a noticeable interaction effect of 0.89 points.

5. OTHER MODELS

Mixed Models

The choice between a fixed or a random model depends on whether we have data on all the categories of the explanatory variables or not. If we have data for all the categories, we use a fixed model; and if we have data for a sample of categories, we use a random model. The choice is most often determined by how easy or difficult it is to collect the data, and it is usually not very difficult to determine which model to use.

However, one difficulty arises when we have two or more explanatory variables and when we have data for all categories of some of them and data on a sample of categories for others. Thus some of the explanatory variables argue for a fixed model while others argue for a random model. The correct model in a case like this is the so-called mixed model, which allows for some fixed and some random effects.

We do not discuss mixed models here, but they are commonly treated in more extensive discussions of analysis of variance.

Three Explanatory Variables

Analysis of variance models generalize directly to three or more categorical, explanatory variables. The main difficulty is that with more variables, there are more effects to keep track of; in particular, the number of interaction effects goes up rapidly. Suppose we have three explanatory variables denoted A, B, and C. Besides three main effects, one for each variable, there are several possible interaction effects. First, each pair of variables gives rise to an interaction effect, resulting in the AB, AC, and BC interactions. Moreover, another interaction effect emerges from the combination of all three variables taken together, called the ABC interaction. That makes a total of four different interaction effects in addition to the three main effects.

The problem is not so much keeping track of the many interaction effects as it is trying to figure out what they mean for the substantive problem under study. Our theories are often not developed well enough for us to know what to make of the higher-order interaction effects among many variables. It is usually desirable to have these interaction effects to be statistically nonsignificant, since they then can be dropped from the model and their sums of squares pooled with the residual sum of squares.

As with the analysis involving two variables, the analysis of more variables requires the explanatory variables to be unrelated if we want separate, unique effects for each of the variables. This is most easily achieved if there are the same numbers of observations for each combination of the explanatory variables. This is only seldom the case for observational data, while it is much easier to achieve for experimental situations.

Latin Square Design

Basic ideas. As we increase the number of explanatory variables, we are faced with the problem of measuring our data under increasingly complex circumstances. In order to make the data gathering less cumbersome and less costly, and perhaps at all feasible, we can avail ourselves of more specialized designs, one of which is called the latin square design.

Suppose the effects of three variables A, B, and C on a dependent variable Y are to be examined, and that each explanatory variable has the same number of categories. In a psychological perception experiment, for example, the color of an object may be one of the explanatory variables, its four categories being red, blue, yellow, and white. The other two variables may be shape and texture, each with four categories. Taken together, the three variables define (4)(4)(4) = 64 different combinations of categories. In order to investigate whether these three variables have any effect on the dependent variable Y, we could set up an experiment to be analyzed by a three-way analysis of variance. With 64 distinct combinations, a minimum of 64 observations would be required, giving only one observation for every combination. A full analysis would require more than one observation for every combination of the explanatory variables. Gathering data under these conditions may be expensive and cumbersome, perhaps making it too difficult to conduct the research.

A latin square design provides a solution to this dilemma. Such a design permits the investigator to study the effects of A, B, and C on Y using only (4)(4) = 16 instead of 64 observations as a minimum for analysis. This reduction is made possible by the assumption that all four interaction effects AB, AC, BC, and ABC are equal to zero. The interaction terms capture the lion's share of degrees of freedom, in this example AB, AC, and BC each being responsible for (4–1)(4–1) = 9 degrees of freedom, and the ABC interaction takes up (4–1)(4–1)(4–1) = 27 degrees of freedom. This adds up to 54 out of a grand total of 63. Only 9 degrees of freedom are used for the effects of the three variables themselves. Once we ignore the interaction effects, we can proceed with a far smaller number of degrees of freedom and, thus, number of observations. If the assumption of no interaction effects is tenable, the use of a latin square design offers great savings in time and effort.

This kind of a saving is obtained by carefully selecting the combinations of the three explanatory variables for which the dependent variable Y is observed. We choose combinations of categories that are balanced in such a way that the effects of A, B, and C can actually be assessed.

Design and analysis. Suppose the categories for variable A are denoted A_1, A_2, A_3, and A_4, and similarly for the other two variables B and C. One possibility is to observe Y for the following set of combinations:

Combinations of A, B and C	Value of Y
$A_1B_1C_1$	y_{111}
$A_1B_2C_4$	y_{124}
$A_1B_3C_3$	y_{133}
$A_1B_4C_2$	y_{142}
$A_2B_1C_2$	y_{212}
$A_2B_2C_1$	y_{221}
$A_2B_3C_4$	y_{234}
$A_2B_4C_3$	y_{243}
$A_3B_1C_3$	y_{313}
$A_3B_2C_2$	y_{322}
$A_3B_3C_1$	y_{331}
$A_3B_4C_4$	y_{344}
$A_4B_1C_4$	y_{414}
$A_4B_2C_3$	y_{423}
$A_4B_3C_2$	y_{432}
$A_4B_4C_1$	y_{441}

The notation for the three subscripts for Y is such that the first subscript refers to the category of the A variable, the second subscript to the category of the B variable, and the third subscript to the category of the C variable.

This list of combinations is not as random as it may seem, and there is a system underlying the selection. The system is such that each category of A occurs once with each category of B and of C; that is, A_1 occurs together with each of the four categories of B as well as with each of the four categories of C, and the same for A_2, A_3, and A_4. The same principle also holds true for the other two variables B and C. It is this kind of balancing of the categories that will make it possible to extract separate and unique sums of squares for the variables A, B, and C. Note that this particular way of combining the categories of the three variables is only one of several ways the categories can be combined.

Another way of displaying the combinations of categories is shown in Table 22. Variable A determines the rows of the table, variable B the columns, and the cells of the table are reserved for variable C. A close look at the table shows that a particular category of C occurs once in each row and each column of the table. This assures that each category of a variable occurs only once with each of the categories of the other variables.

The bottom part of the table shows numerical values of the dependent variable Y for each of the 16 cells of the design, here one observation per cell. We now turn to the question of how to assess the effects of the three variables A, B, and C on Y. The values of Y are not alike because they have been affected by A, B, C, and the residual variable, and the degree to which the observations are different is measured by the total sum of squares, TSS. Here we have

$$TSS = \Sigma(y_{ijk} - \overline{y})^2 = 271.42$$

with 15 degrees of freedom, since there are 16 observations.

In order to find how much A, B, and C have contributed to this sum, we must first find the mean of Y for each of the categories of A, B, and C. Since each of the three variables has four categories, we must compute 12 different means. Let us start with the mean of Y for the first category of A. The category A_1, occurs with the four observations in the first row of the table, and their mean is

$$\overline{y}_{1..} = (y_{111} + y_{124} + y_{133} + y_{142})/4$$
$$= (12.0 + 10.5 + 10.7 + 11.2)/4 = 11.10$$

Since the first subscript refers to the A variable and we are finding the mean for the first category of A, we denote this mean $\overline{y}_{1..}$, with dots placed in the second and third subscript to indicate that we have added up over those subscripts for B and C. Similarly, we find

$$\overline{y}_{2..} = 12.22 \qquad \overline{y}_{3..} = 12.15 \qquad \overline{y}_{4..} = 4.52$$

These means are different, indicating that A has an effect. To measure that effect we subtract the overall mean of 10.00 from each of the four group means, square the differences, multiply each difference by the number of observations in the group (4), and add these products. That gives the following sum of squares for the A variable,

$$SSA = 4(11.10 - 10.00)^2 + 4(12.22 - 10.00)^2$$
$$+ 4(12.15 - 10.00)^2 + 4(4.52 - 10.00)^2$$
$$= 163.04$$

TABLE 22
Combinations of Categories Used in a Latin Square Design, with Data

	B_1	B_2	B_3	B_4
A_1	C_1	C_4	C_3	C_2
A_2	C_2	C_1	C_4	C_3
A_3	C_3	C_2	C_1	C_4
A_4	C_4	C_3	C_2	C_1

					Means
	12.0	10.5	10.7	11.2	11.10
	15.9	10.3	15.2	7.5	12.22
	12.7	11.2	13.6	11.1	12.15
	7.7	0.1	8.6	1.7	4.52
Means	12.08	8.02	12.02	7.88	10.00

The sum of squares for B is found in a similar way. B has an effect if the means for the four categories of B are different. These means are found as the four column means, and they are different. The magnitude of the differences is measured by subtracting the overall mean from each of the four group means, squaring each difference, and multiplying each square by 4. The sum of squares for B is found by adding these products, that is,

$$SSB = \Sigma 4(\overline{y}_{.j.} - \overline{y})^2 = 67.29$$

The sum of squares for C is more cumbersome to find because the means for the different categories of C are not as apparent in the data table as the means for A and B. In order to find the mean of the four observations for C_1, we see that this category occurs for the observations that are located on the diagonal in the table running from the upper left to the lower right. The mean of these observations gives us $\overline{y}_{..1} = 9.40$. Similarly, for $\overline{y}_{..2}$ we collect the four observations that refer to C_2, and the same procedure is followed for the other two means. The effect of variable C is measured the same way as for A and B, and we get

$$SSC = \Sigma 4(\overline{y}_{..k} - \overline{y})^2 = 38.66$$

The residual sum of squares is found by subtracting the sums of squares for A, B, and C from the total sum of squares. The various sums of squares with their degrees of freedom, mean squares, and F-ratios are shown in Table 23. All three variables have significant effects, and together they account for almost all the variation in Y.

The advantage of a latin square design is that it makes it possible to assess the effects of several explanatory variables by observing a smaller number of observations than the total number of combinations of the explanatory variables. In this example we need only 16 observations, even though the three variables define a total of 64 possible combinations. But this procedure is only permitted if all the interaction effects can be assumed to be insignificant. Violations of this assumption call the use of a latin square design into question (Winer, 1971: 514-538).

Nested Designs

A variety of designs for collecting and analyzing data exist beyond those discussed above. From among the remaining designs we mention the nested design, sometimes also called hierarchical design. In its most simple form the nested design is an incomplete two-way design. It is incomplete in the sense that not all the data are available which would allow for a two-way analysis the way such an analysis is discussed in Chapters 3 and 4.

As an example of data calling for a nested design, take congressional districts organized within those states with more than one district. If we were to assess the effect of district versus the effect of state level forces on some dependent variable, we would construct a design in which the districts were nested within their respective states. Since a given district is located only in one state, the two explanatory variables district and state cannot be completely crossed the way the two explanatory variables were crossed in Chapter 3. Table 24 presents a fragment of the nested design, listing three states S_1, S_2, and S_3 with three congressional districts nested within each state. Within each district n individuals are observed on the dependent variable Y. The notation for y_{ijk} is such that the first subscript refers to state, the second to district, and the third to individual.

A nested design in conjunction with a random model was employed by Stokes (1965, 1967) in his study of electoral effects. Voting turnout as well as the party division in congressional elections were observed across

TABLE 23
Analysis of Variance Table for Latin Square Example

Source	Sum of Squares	Degrees of Freedom	Mean Square	F-ratio	Significance
A	163.04	3	54.34	509.80	0.0000
B	67.29	3	22.43	55.15	0.0001
C	38.66	3	12.88	31.69	0.0004
Residual	2.44	6	0.41		
Total	271.43	15			

TABLE 24
Form of the Data for a Nested Design

Congressional District

State	C_1	C_2	C_3	C_4	C_5	C_6	C_7	C_8	C_9
S_1	y_{111} y_{112} $\vdots$ y_{11n}	y_{121} y_{122} $\vdots$ y_{12n}	y_{131} y_{132} $\vdots$ y_{13n}						
S_2				y_{241} y_{242} $\vdots$ y_{24n}	y_{251} y_{252} $\vdots$ y_{25n}	y_{261} y_{262} $\vdots$ y_{26n}			
S_3							y_{371} y_{372} $\vdots$ y_{37n}	y_{381} y_{382} $\vdots$ y_{38n}	y_{391} y_{392} $\vdots$ y_{39n}

time for districts, states, and the nation as a whole. The purpose of the analysis was to separate out the effects due to district, state, and national forces as they bear on voting turnout and the partisan division of the vote. Stokes presents the variance components for the three effects and compares their sizes across a long historical span, noting striking trends in the variations of these effects over time.

Analysis of Variance and Regression

A final comment is devoted to the relationship between analysis of variance and regression analysis. These models are closely related because they are both special cases of the so-called general linear model. Regression is treated in more detail in several other papers in this series, and we merely intend to hint at two aspects of the interface between the two models.

Both regression and analysis of variance. The first issue we raise is the question of what happens if we apply both methods to the same data. When there are several values of the dependent variable Y for each value of the independent variable X and X is a metric variable, then it is possible to do analysis of variance as well as regression. An illustration of data of this kind is shown in the top of Table 25, where there are five different values of X and for each X there are from two to five values of Y. As an example, let X measure media use on a scale from 1 to 5, and Y is the rating score of the importance of the economy.

Since X is a metric variable, regression analysis would seem like the proper model for the analysis of the relationship between X and Y. The results of such a regression analysis are shown just below the data in Table 25. The slope is positive, the relationship is fairly strong, and the relationship is very significant. Since there is only one X variable, the degrees of freedom split up with 1 for the regression and as many as 13 for the residual, measuring how well the regression model fits.

It is also possible to do a one-way analysis of variance on these data. In that case we look at these data as simply arranged in five different groups. We make no use of the fact that X is a metric variable, which provides a strong ordering of the groups from small to large values of X. By giving up this fact we are not using all the information in the data, and the penalty for this turns out to be that we must use more degrees of freedom for the model, leaving fewer for the residual.

The results from the analysis of variance are shown in the middle of Table 25. The total sums of squares and degrees of freedom are the same as for the regression analysis, but they are allocated differently. In

TABLE 25
Both Regression and Analysis of Variance

Data:	X:	1	2	3	4	5
	Y:	4	5	6	6	8
		3	4	5	7	10
		2	3	4	8	
				3		

Regression analysis: $Y = 1.03 + 1.45X$ $R^2 = 52.35/70.40 = 0.75$

Source	Sum of Squares	Degrees of Freedom	Mean Square	F-ratio	Significance
Regression	52.35	1	52.35	33.95	0.00006
Residual	20.05	13	1.54		
Total	70.40	14			

Analysis of variance: $eta^2 = 59.40/70.40 = 0.84$

Groups	59.40	4	14.85	11.42	0.001
Residual	13.00	10	1.30		
Total	70.40	14			

Combined:

Regression	52.35	1	52.35	40.27	0.0001
Deviation from line	7.05	3	2.35	1.81	0.21
Residual	13.00	10	1.30		
Total	72.40	14			

particular, the residual sum of squares is smaller for the analysis of variance, indicating that the analysis of variance model fits better than the regression model. On the other hand, the regression model requires only 1 degree of freedom, while the analysis of variance model requires 4 degrees of freedom. The net effect of the different sums of squares and degrees of freedom is that the F for the regression is much more significant than the F for analysis of variance. Thus, if the analysis is done for the purpose of seeing whether a relationship is significant, regression is the better model to use.

But since the analysis of variance fits better, it gives the stronger relationship. Measuring the strength of the relationship, we find that with regression we get R^2 equal to 0.75, while for analysis of variance we get eta^2 equal to 0.84. The fact that the relationship is stronger using analysis of variance is simply a reflection of the fact that analysis of variance uses 4 degrees of freedom and regression only 1. In general, the more degrees of freedom a model uses for the study of a relationship between two variables, the better the model fits and the stronger the relationship becomes. But the fewer degrees of freedom a model uses, the more parsimonious it is and the better it helps us understand the nature of the relationship.

Aside from comparing the two methods, there is another reason for doing both analyses. Together they permit us to examine whether the relationship between X and Y is linear or not. The regression model assumes a linear relationship, but many times we do no more than casually look at a scatterplot to see if the assumption is true. The reason we now can do more has to do with the residuals. In regression they are measured as deviations from the regression line, whereas in analysis of variance they are measured as deviations from the group means. If the regression line passes through all the group means, then the residuals will be the same for the two analyses. But when the relationship is not linear, the regression line will not pass through the group means, and the two sets of residuals will be different. In particular, the residuals around the regression line will produce a larger sum of squares than the residuals around the group means.

By comparing the results from the two analyses, we find that the two residual sums of squares differ by 7.05. They differ because the group means do not lie on the regression line. In the bottom part of Table 25 this difference is entered as "deviation from line" sum of squares along with the residual sum of squares from the analysis of variance and the regression sum of squares from the regression analysis. The 4 degrees of freedom from the analysis of variance have been allocated with 1 for the linear relationship, as found by the regression analysis, and 3 for the nonlinear part of the relationship. That gives us the mean squares and F-ratios in the combined table, showing a very significant linear relationship and a nonsignificant deviation from linearity.

Regression instead of analysis of variance. Data studied by analysis of variance can always be studied using regression analysis with suitably constructed dummy variables. Any categorical variable can be represented by a set of dummy variables; and even though it may be cumbersome to set up the dummy variables, the regression software may be easier to use than analysis of variance software. For a much more

TABLE 26
Dummy Variables for Data in Table 3

Group	Y	D_1	D_2	D_3	D_4
A	6	1	0	0	0
	6	1	0	0	0
	6	1	0	0	0
	8	1	0	0	0
	9	1	0	0	0
B	7	0	1	0	0
	8	0	1	0	0
	8	0	1	0	0
	8	0	1	0	0
	9	0	1	0	0
C	4	0	0	1	0
	4	0	0	1	0
	5	0	0	1	0
	6	0	0	1	0
	6	0	0	1	0
D	5	0	0	0	1
	5	0	0	0	1
	6	0	0	0	1
	6	0	0	0	1
	8	0	0	0	1
E	3	0	0	0	0
	4	0	0	0	0
	4	0	0	0	0
	4	0	0	0	0
	5	0	0	0	0

extensive discussion of the correspondence between the two sets of models, see Edwards (1979).

As an illustration, let us go back to the data in Table 3 used for the comparison of several groups in the one-way analysis of variance and do a regression analysis instead. Since there are 5 groups of observations, we need 4 dummy variables for the analysis. The assignment of zeros and ones for the dummy variables are shown in Table 26.

A multiple regression of Y on the four variables D_1, D_2, D_3, and D_4 results in the estimated regression equation

$$Y = 4.0 + 3.0D_1 + 4.0D_2 + 1.0D_3 + 2.0D_4$$

The sums of squares and degrees of freedom for this analysis are identical to those shown for the analysis of variance in Table 5. Since there are four explanatory variables in this regression analysis, we get four degrees of freedom for the regression sum of squares of 12.50. Since the sums of squares are the same in the two analyses, we also get that eta square is equal to R square. In short, there are no differences between the results of the two analyses. The use of dummy variables works equally well for two-way analyses of variance.

The choice of method of analysis comes down to a question of convenience. Depending on how the data file is set up or the availability of computer software, one analysis may be easier to perform than another. The choice may also depend on personal preference, some people find regression analysis more appealing while others prefer analysis of variance.

6. CONCLUSIONS

Review

We entered into the discussion of the method known as analysis of variance (ANOVA) by way of a substantive question. The question dealt with the effect the mass media may have on the public's concern with the economy. Let us now review to what extent ANOVA has helped us answer that basic question. The data came from hypothetical experiments.

One-way ANOVA, employing what is called a fixed model, has applied a test of the (null) hypothesis that television newscasts have no effect on how important people rate the economy as an issue. An experimental group viewed a newscast containing a story on the economy, while a control group viewed the same newscast minus the economy story; participants of both groups were randomly assigned to the groups. The results showed a highly significant F-ratio, which meant that the null hypothesis was rejected. We conclude that television newscasts raise the public's concern with the economy.

But do they do equally so for the key economic issues, namely unemployment and inflation, and does it matter whether the news is good or bad for each of these issues? These questions call for an extension on the one-way to a two-way ANOVA. Now, the economic issue (unemployment, inflation) forms one explanatory variable, while the valence of the news coverage (positive, negative) forms the other. By randomly assigning the subjects to one of the four conditions created by crossing the two variables, we are able to eliminate the systematic effect of all other variables. Moreover, by assigning the same number of subjects to each condition, we make certain that the two explanatory variables are uncorrelated with each other. Only with equal, or unequal but proportional, cell frequencies can we proceed in a straightforward fashion to estimate the unique effect of each explanatory variable on the dependent variable, test for the significance of each, and estimate the proportion of the overall variation due to each explanatory variable.

Two-way ANOVA also introduces a concept not known in a one-way analysis: the concept of interaction. This refers to the way in which a category of one explanatory variable combines with a category of the other explanatory variable to produce an effect on the dependent variable that goes beyond the sum of the separate effects. In this example the analysis shows that when the news is negative, unemployment and inflation stories create the same concern in the public with the economy. But when the news is positive, only unemployment stories create little concern, while inflation stories still generate moderate levels of concern.

Interaction is a feature common in both experimental and observational studies. In addition, observational studies typically confront the researcher with correlated explanatory variables. This correlation complicates two-way ANOVA, which was not designed with that condition in mind. In using two-way ANOVA on data with correlated explanatory variables, the analyst must decide which of the explanatory variables is to be entered into the analysis first. As in royal families, being first carries considerable privilege. In ANOVA it bestows the shared explanatory variation to the variable entered first, with the result that the variable entered second will prove less significant than if it came first; at worst, its effect is no longer statistically significant. With correlated variables two-way ANOVA leaves us out on a limb with two sets of estimated effects to choose from. To decide we must reach for metastatistical considerations.

These considerations are illustrated with data from a hypothetical sample survey on the salience of the economy among blacks and whites and depending on whether one personally suffered unemployment or not. Neither of these conditions lends itself to experimental manipulation, and they are plainly correlated with each other. The sums of squares, as estimates of the effects of race and unemployment, are shown to change sharply depending on which of the two takes the first crack at explaining the importance ratings of the economy.

Having grappled with the intricacies of correlated variables, also known as a nonorthogonal design, we took on what is known as the random model. Whatever the differences of ANOVA considered so far, all those versions conform to the fixed model, where data are available for all categories of the explanatory variable. In research situations where this is not feasible, the random model comes to the rescue. Now the researcher has to obtain a random sample of categories, and then for each of the chosen categories a random sample of respondents is chosen. The need for a sample of categories arises in studies of the effect of something that occurs in almost limitless permutations, such as orderings of questions in a questionnaire. Salience ratings of the economy, for example, may very well depend on where among other items this question is placed, with possibly damaging consequences for the substantive conclusions.

Both the fixed and random models make certain assumptions which we noted on several occasions. These assumptions, however, need not always be met in the strictest sense of their meanings. Sometimes they can be moderately violated without the results losing their theoretical justification.

The assumption of a normal distribution of the residuals for each category or combination of categories of the explanatory variable(s) is one of them. This assumption need not bother us greatly as long as the sample of observations for each category is relatively large. This goes for both the fixed and the random model, as far as they were presented, although departures from normality are to be taken more seriously in the latter case. The random model, moreover, also requires the effects to be normally distributed. To secure large sample sizes of respondents would seem an easier job for survey studies than for experiments.

A second assumption worth our attention concerns the variance of the residual term. This variance is supposed to be constant for all categories or combination of categories of the explanatory variable(s). This assumption can be explicitly tested; but even when it is found lacking, the analysis is not necessarily doomed. This holds true, for example, in one-way analysis employing a fixed model as long as the number of observations is approximately equal for all categories. Whereas the planning of experiments typically can assure such equality, survey studies are less equipped to do so.

Other Topics

This short introduction to analysis of variance covers the major issues and leaves other topics to further studies. Throughout the discussion we have stated what assumptions the data have to satisfy in order to do the analysis, but we have left out a more detailed treatment of what happens if the assumptions are not satisfied. We have not discussed what is known as multiple comparison procedures, which enable us to compare subsets of group means after the null hypothesis of equal means has been rejected. Furthermore, with unequal number of observations in the groups, we have correlated explanatory variables, and we give only a brief introduction to the solution of this problem. We do not explicitly discuss the so-called repeated measurement designs, where several observations have been made on a single unit (individual). These observations can be taken together as a block of observations, and the variations in the individuals can be taken out of the residual sum of squares. It is also worth mentioning that we give only a limited discussion of the treatment of interactions. For a more detailed discussion of these and other issues, we refer to the textbooks in the references or other texts on analysis of variance.

REFERENCES

ANSCOMBE, F. J. and J. W. TUKEY (1963) "The examination and analysis of residuals." Techometrics 5, no. 2 (May): 141-160.

BLOOM, H. S. and H. D. PRICE (1975) "Voter response to short-run economic conditions: The asymmetric effect of prosperity and recession." American Political Science Review 69: 1240-1254.

COBB, G. (1984) "An algorithmic approach to elementary ANOVA." The American Statistician 38 (May): 120-123.

COCHRAN, W. G. (1965) "The planning of observational studies of human populations." J. of the Royal Statistical Society, series A, 128, part 2: 234-265.

———(1983) Planning and Analysis of Observational Studies. New York: Wiley

COCHRAN, W. G. and G. COX (1957) Experimental Designs. New York: Wiley.

EDWARDS, A. F. (1979) Multiple Regression and the Analysis of Variance and Covariance. San Francisco: W. H. Freeman.

HAYS, W. J. (1981) Statistics, 3rd ed. New York: Holt, Rinehart & Winston.

IYENGAR, S. and D. R. KINDER (1987) News that Matters: Television and American Opinion. Chicago: Chicago University Press.

KERNELL, S. (1977) "Presidential popularity and negative voting." American Political Science Review 71: 44-66.

LANOUE, D. (1986) Understanding Presidential Popularity in the United States: Prosperity and Partisanship. Ph.D. dissertation, SUNY at Stony Brook.

PETERSEN, R. G. (1986) Design and Analysis of Experiments. New York: Marcel Dekker.

SCHEFFÉ, H. (1959) The Analysis of Variance. New York: Wiley.

SNEDECOR, G. W. and W. G. COCHRAN (1967) Statistical Methods. Ames: Iowa State Univ. Press.
STOKES, D. E. (1965) "A variance components model of political effects," in J. M. Claunch (ed.). Mathematical Applications in Political Science. Dallas: Arnold Foundation, 61-85.
———(1967) "Parties and the nationalization of electoral forces," in W. N. Chambers and W. D. Burnham (eds.). The American Party Systems. New York: Oxford Univ. Press, 182-202.
WINER, B. J. (1971) Statistical Principles in Experimental Design. New York: McGraw-Hill.

GUDMUND R. IVERSEN, *Professor of Statistics and a statistician at the Center for Social and Policy Studies, Swarthmore College, received his Ph.D. in statistics from Harvard University. His articles have appeared in several scholarly journals, including* Public Opinion Quarterly, Psychometrika, World Politics, American Journal of Sociology, *and* American Statistician. *He is the author of an introductory statistics text for sociology and a coauthor of a book on statistical analysis of individual and group data in addition to the text on Bayesian statistical inference in this series.*

HELMUT NORPOTH, *Professor of Political Science at the State University of New York, Stony Brook, received his Ph.D. in political science from the University of Michigan. His articles have appeared in several scholarly journals, including* American Political Science Review, American Journal of Political Science Review, *and* Political Behavior. *His work deals largely with public opinion and electoral behavior.*

NOTES

NOTES